Handcrafting
Chain and
Bead Jewelry

Handcrafting
Chain and
Bead Jewelry

Techniques for Creating
Dimensional Necklaces and Bracelets

Scott David Plumlee

Watson-Guptill Publications/New York

First published in 2006 by
Watson-Guptill Publications,
Nielsen Business Media, a division of The Nielsen Company
770 Broadway, New York, N.Y. 10003
www.watsonguptill.com

All projects by Scott David Plumlee
All jewelry photography by Scott David Plumlee
All step by step photography by Lisa Eastman

Library of Congress Cataloging-in-Publication Data

Plumlee, Scott David.
Handcrafting chain and bead jewelry : techniques for creating dimensional necklaces and bracelets / Scott David Plumlee.
p. cm.
Includes index.
ISBN-13: 978-0-8230-2299-1
ISBN-10: 0-8230-2299-4
1. Jewelry making. 2. Metalwork. 3. Beadwork. 4.
Chains (Jewelry) I. Title.
TT212.P55 22006
745.594'2—dc22

2006004438

Senior Acquisitions Editor: Joy Aquilino
Editors: Anne McNamara and John A. Foster
Designer: Pooja Bakri
Senior Production Manager: Ellen Greene

Manufactured in Malaysia

First printing, 2006

4 5 6 7 8 9 / 14 13 12 11 10 09 08 07

A Note to Readers:

When working with pliers, electric screwdrivers, wire, and other materials presented in this book, readers are strongly cautioned to follow manufacturers' directions, to heed warnings, and to seek prompt medical attention for an injury. In addition, readers are advised to keep all potentially harmful supplies away from children.

Contents

Preface

Welcome to my world, where art and science merge, creating endless possibilities for dynamic chain jewelry! The chain-making techniques illustrated in this book utilize simple hand tools, thus freeing artists from the confines of the metalworking studio.

During my singular jewelry course, I studied the finer techniques of silversmithing, from soldering bezel settings to using a variety of power tools. Upon completing a spinning triptych pendant, I realized that the product appeared sterile—made by machine, not by hand. Furthermore, I felt that power tools were quite loud, and on account of their dependency on electricity, hindered my creativity and mobility.

When I set off to travel around the world in 1996, I craved a portable craft that would provide a satisfying artistic outlet. I chose to embrace the elements of silversmithing I enjoyed and to reject the rest. I gave up my crutch of studio and hot torch for a quiet, hands-on, instantly gratifying, and meditative process. For the greater part of five years, I traveled across thirty-two countries on four continents. I utilized my chain-making skills to influence border guards, to barter for goods and services, and to provide gifts to family, friends, and a few pretty ladies along my path.

When I settled in Seattle, Washington, I went back to the blackboard to develop a mathematical formula based on the Golden Ratio of Pi (3.14) that utilized individual wire gauge to determine the ideal diameter for jump rings. The jump rings I made with this formula produced chains of physical linear strength and eliminated the necessity of soldering each ring. This new method opened the door to a whole new world of creative possibilities, which eventually led me to develop over sixty unique chain designs.

In 2001, I began teaching chain-making workshops. I developed handouts with step-by-step instructions to guide my students through the chain-making process. These handouts eventually became the basis for this book, and conversely this book would not have been conceivable without these teaching experiences.

The opening section of the book describes the foundations of the classic Byzantine chain. Then a selection of original chain designs, based on the Byzantine, is introduced and accompanied with bead-setting techniques. These chain designs are divided into four chapters: Linear Designs, Additive Designs, Combined Designs, and Composed Designs.

The projects should be seen as building blocks, each introducing skills that can be carried through to the next project.

While my desire is to share with you the knowledge and skills that I have acquired over the years, my ambition, above all else, is for you to have fun with this book—share it with a friend, even take it on a vacation. Go to a Caribbean beach and chain away the sunsets. . . .

The Byzantine Chain

This book is dedicated to unraveling the mysteries of the Sequential Byzantine chain. All fifteen original chain designs outlined in this book are derivatives of this ancient chain pattern. The origin of the Byzantine chain is a mystery; I have seen slight variations of it all over the globe. It is known by many different names to many different civilizations.

I was first introduced to the Byzantine chain while I was an undergraduate studying pottery and silversmithing at the Appalachian Center for Crafts in Tennessee. I found in their eclectic library an old Taiwanese text with no translation and only hand-drawn pictures of a beautiful chain pattern. After countless hours toiling with lopsided rings, a half-dozen botched chains, and the angst of trial and error, I eventually developed an efficient motion for making this chain, yet I didn't know its name.

Since then, I have seen this chain pattern labeled the Byzantine or, more specifically, the Sequential Byzantine chain, in numerous publications. I can only assume that this is a reference to the thirteenth-century Byzantine Empire. I've also seen several books that label this chain pattern as the Idiot's Delight or, more specifically, as the Sequential Link Idiot's Delight. Although I really like this name, I always thought it would be difficult to market a workshop on handcrafting the Idiot's Delight, so I kept with the more universally recognized Byzantine designation.

The three Byzantine chains pictured above were made using sizes 14-, 16-, and 18-gauge jump rings, shown from left to right. These are the three gauge sizes used to create the designs in this book.

The Inca Puño Chain

While trekking through South America, I witnessed a blacksmith crafting a repetitive chain. He salvaged copper wire by unbraiding old electrical cables. After a charcoal annealing, he pulled the red-hot wire through a drawplate to create a 16-gauge round wire. He then wrapped the cooled wire around a hand-whittled wooden dowel and cut it with a small handsaw. What amazed me most was that he did not use pliers to bend the rings, just his calloused fingertips. I learned that in Spanish this chain was known as the *Inca puño*. Puño translates as "a clenched fist," and each knot in this repetitive chain represents the clenched fist of the Incan warrior. It traditionally is given as a mark of courage to the young men in a tribe.

The Inca puño chain is a repetitive chain pattern that holds the key building block of the Byzantine chain. It is based on a repetition of four jump rings, assembled 2+2, and then folded into a knot formation. Each knot is connected, and held in folded form, to its neighboring knots. The Inca puño chain differs from the Byzantine chain in being a repetitive chain sequence of knot formations without any connector pairs in between.

The Inca puño chain is based on the key knot formation of the Byzantine chain.

The Double Chain

The double chain is also a repetitive chain pattern based on a simple two-ring on two-ring sequence. This chain sequence is the second building block of the Byzantine chain. Two parallel rings are utilized as connector pairs within the Byzantine chain to increase the chain's strength in resisting linear tension. The double chain differs from the Byzantine chain in that it is a repetitive sequence of connector pairs without any knot formations in between.

The double chain has the same repetitive two-ring on two-ring sequence that the Byzantine chain utilizes as connector pairs.

Utilizing Pi

$$\pi = 3.14159265358979323846264338327950288\,4197\ldots\ldots$$

The symbol above, known as *Pi*, is the sixteenth letter of the Greek alphabet and the mathematical symbol that represents the number 3.14, an irrational number that extends to infinity.

Within the realm of simple Euclidian geometry, Pi is used to find the circumference of a circle by multiplying the circle's diameter by Pi.

The Byzantine chain is made by utilizing Pi as a multiplier to determine the proper ratio of wire to jump ring. When the round wire's diameter is multiplied by Pi, the result is the inside diameter of the jump ring.

The inside diameter of the jump ring as determined by the Pi formula will give you the diameter of the mandrel you should use for wrapping the wire into a coil (*see* Wire Skills on page 27). Conversely, the mandrel's diameter will be the same as the coil's inside diameter, so that when the coil is cut into jump rings, each jump ring will have the same inside diameter.

In the United States, round wire is typically measured and sold in diameter increments called *gauges*. In Canada and Europe, round wire is measured and sold by diameter increments in quarter-millimeters. The chain designs in this book use three gauges of round wire: 18, 16, and 14.

When the round wire's diameter is multiplied by Pi, the result is the inside diameter of the jump ring.

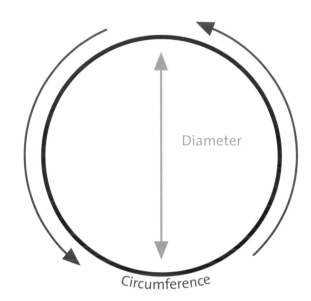

Diameter

Circumference

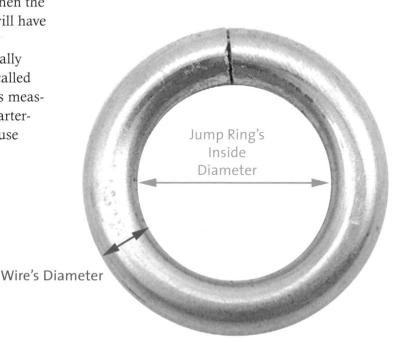

Jump Ring's Inside Diameter

Wire's Diameter

In order to determine the proper inside diameter of the jump rings and mandrel size you will need in order to make each chain, look at the three tables to the right. (Since round wire is sold by gauges in the United States, the metric diameter size is placed in parentheses.) Each round wire's diameter is then multiplied by a specific multiplier, depending on the type of chain you are creating. For example, you would multiply the wire's diameter by 3.14 to find the jump ring and mandrel sizes for a Byzantine chain; by 4 for the the Inca puño chain; and by 2.5 for the Double chain.

Close inspection of these charts reveals that one mandrel can be used to wrap different sizes of wire, each of which, in turn, produces a different chain. For example, the 4.00mm mandrel will wrap the 18-gauge wire for the Inca puño chain, the 16-gauge wire for the Byzantine chain, and the 14-gauge wire for the double chain. If you are using 16-gauge wire, you would use a 3.25mm mandrel to make a Double jump ring, a 5.25mm mandrel to make an Inca puño jump ring, and a 4.00mm mandrel to make a Byzantine jump ring.

I cannot stress enough that the precise inside diameter of the jump rings, which is determined by the mandrel, is critical for these chains to work. If the rings are too small in diameter, they will not allow the chain to complete the folding action. If the rings are too large in diameter, the chain will be too loose, creating a sloppy and weak chain. (*See* Evaluating Chains on page 51 for more on this topic.)

Note: If you are using plastic-coated copper wire, the flush-cutting technique, or a jeweler's saw to cut jump rings, you will need to add a quarter-millimeter to the mandrel size.

BYZANTINE CHAIN

Gauge (dia.mm)	Metric Size	Multiply by 3.14	Jump Ring inside dia.	Mandrel Size
	1.00	3.14	3.14	3.25
18 (1.02)		3.14	3.20	3.25
	1.25	3.14	3.93	4.00
16 (1.29)		3.14	4.05	4.00
	1.50	3.14	4.71	4.75
14 (1.63)		3.14	5.12	5.25
	1.75	3.14	5.50	5.50

INCA PUÑO CHAIN

Gauge (dia.mm)	Metric Size	Multiply by 4	Jump Ring inside dia.	Mandrel Size
	1.00	4	4.00	4.00
18 (1.02)		4	4.08	4.00
	1.25	4	5.00	5.00
16 (1.29)		4	5.16	5.25
	1.50	4	6.00	6.00
14 (1.63)		4	6.52	6.50
	1.75	4	7.00	7.00

DOUBLE CHAIN

Gauge (dia.mm)	Metric Size	Multiply by 2.5	Jump Ring inside dia.	Mandrel Size
	1.00	2.5	2.50	2.50
18 (1.02)		2.5	2.55	2.50
	1.25	2.5	3.13	3.25
16 (1.29)		2.5	3.23	3.25
	1.50	2.5	3.75	3.75
14 (1.63)		2.5	4.08	4.00
	1.75	2.5	4.38	4.50

Getting
Started

This section introduces some of the basic tools and skills that you will need to begin making chain and bead jewelry. First, we discuss the various tools needed to manipulate and cut wire. Then we review the basic materials required for chain making and setting beads. Next we go through the wire skills needed to create the chain designs in this book. I will show you step by step how to coil wire, cut jump rings, forge clasps, make earring backings, and, finally, how to assemble and evaluate chains.

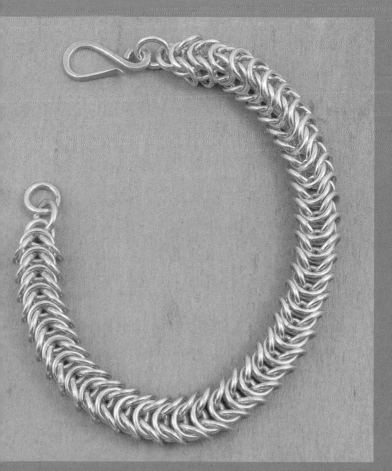

Tools and Supplies

On the following pages, I will introduce the tools and basic materials needed for chain making: wire and beads. For mobility, I recommend wrapping a quantity of round wire into coils, which can later be cut into jump rings. Wrapping the coils ahead of time accomplishes three things: (1) compacts the metal's space, (2) allows you to leave the wrapping tools at home, and (3) prevents the soft wire from getting mangled and bent during travel. Likewise, for the clasp and catch rings needed to complete each bracelet or necklace, you can either buy a quantity of pre made clasps and catch rings, or hammer your own S-clasps.

Tools

The chain-making techniques illustrated in this book utilize simple hand tools, which allow the utmost freedom of mobility and eliminate the risk of dangerous power tools. Bear in mind that most of the tools presented can be left at home after some initial preparations are completed.

Mandrels

Round aluminum knitting needles come in a wide variety of sizes and are easy to find at local knitting and fabric stores. Because they increase in size by somewhat precise quarter-millimeter increments, they serve uncommonly well as mandrels for wrapping wire. To make jump rings for the Byzantine chain, I recommend purchasing 7-inch, double-pointed aluminum knitting needles, which are sold in packets of four. Do not use bamboo or plastic knitting needles, nails, or wooden dowels, as they have uneven diameters and are unreliable in surface and strength. For easy reference, you can color-code your stock of knitting-needle mandrels using different-colored fingernail polishes.

If you cannot find the mandrel size you need, there are several alternatives. Phillips-head screwdriver shafts work great. Drill a small hole that is the size of the wire into the handle in order to hold the coil's spring tension while hand wrapping. Drill bits are available in diameters that increase in smaller increments; however, you cannot wrap wire over the spiral-cutting surface of the bit, only over the round stock. You can also search welding supply shops for round steel stock, which drill bits are made from, and request a 7-inch section.

Above left: Aluminum knitting needles come in a variety of sizes and make ideal mandrels for wrapping wire. Below left: Never trust a package's U.S. number size or millimeter size; instead, always open the package and measure the knitting needles with a digital caliper. Digital calipers can be purchased inexpensively at craft and hardware stores.

Side Cutters

Side cutters are available at jewelry supply shops in lengths from 4½ to 6 inches with angled cutting blades. Cutters are rated on the maximum gauge size that the blades can cut; the smaller side cutter pictured on the far left is rated to cut 18 gauge, while the larger side cutter is rated for 14 gauge. Keep in mind that you get what you pay for. Because you use only the tips of the cutters, cheaper cutters will dull more quickly and warp out of alignment, making sloppy cuts. Get the best cutters you can afford and take good care of them; it will make a difference in the quality of your jump rings and chain.

3.6-volt Cordless Screwdriver

This modern marvel is 9 inches in length and quite portable at 2 pounds. Let me clarify that this is a cordless screwdriver that runs on a 3.6-volt battery, not a cordless drill that runs on an 18-volt battery. Do not attempt to wrap wire with any type of drill; they have way more speed and torque than what is required and can be quite dangerous. Available at your local hardware store, Black & Decker manufactures several affordable 3.6-volt models that are powered with a rechargeable nickel cadmium battery. When fully charged with the AC adaptor, this battery will last a long time.

Three-Prong Chuck

All cordless screwdrivers have a hexagon-shaped bit holder, so you will need a three-prong chuck adapter. Technically, this item is called a quarter-inch hexagon-shaped snap-out drill chuck, and is available at hardware stores or online (*see* Resources on page 126). This chuck is necessary to hold the mandrel while wrapping. The space between the three prongs holds the end of the wire and maintains the tension.

Magnifier

Magnifiers are available at hobby and jewelry supply shops. The string wraps around your neck, and the magnifying lens rests perpendicularly against your chest for hands-free chain making without eyestrain. Luckily for me I'm nearsighted. However, if you're not—get some magnification!

Measuring Tape

Measuring tapes are available at knitting and sewing stores. The flexible nature of this plastic tape makes it ideal for measuring wire lengths, overall chain lengths, and the wearer's wrist or neckline (*see* Length on page 51).

Digital Caliper

Available at jewelry supply stores, this instrument displays both millimeters and inches to the hundredth decimal place. It's ideal for measuring the diameter of wire, knitting needle mandrels, and the inside diameter of jump rings. This modern marvel replaces many measuring devices and is quite mobile, as it is battery powered and can be stored in a protective case.

Bandanna

Fold a bandanna to fit the palm of your hand in order to reduce tension and friction when wrapping and straightening wire. If a bandanna is not available, any scrap of cloth will do.

4oz Ball-Peen Hammer

Ball-peen hammers are available at hardware stores with a ⅝-inch wide round head and a half-domed back side. Jewelers' chasing or planishing hammers will work, but they are usually lighter in weight and have too large of a head for working 14-gauge wire, making it difficult to see the work in progress. However, forging S-clasps is more about hand-eye coordination and applied pressure than the type of hammer utilized, so feel free to use whatever type you have.

Bench Block Anvil

Available through a jewelry supply shop, this square ¾-inch-thick steel plate measures 4 x 4 inches. It is ideal for small chasing projects such as the S-clasp (*see* page 36) and the Spade design (*see* page 68).

3M Foam Sanding Pad

Available at hardware stores or jewelry supply shops, these square sanding pads measure 4 x 5 inches, are made of foam rubber bonded with aluminum oxide abrasives, and are designed for wet or dry sanding. They are sold in many grades, but I recommend getting the 320-grit superfine and 600-grit ultrafine grade. These pads are ideal for smoothing the forged tongue points of the S-clasp (*see* page 36) and Spade design (*see* page 68) after needle file shaping. They also can be placed under the bench block while hammering to dampen the noise and keep the anvil from sliding across the table.

Emery Sanding Paper

Available at hardware stores, this paper is designed for wet-sanding metal with a waterproof-backed and silicon carbide abrasive. Use several grit grades from 1000-grit (1/0-grade) to 2000-grit (4/0-grade) to remove any scratches from the hammerhead, as blemishes will transfer to the forging metal. Place the sanding paper on top of a thick telephone book; this cushion will give a slightly rounded head. With a little bit of water, work the metal from coarser to finer grits until you have a mirror shine (*see* photo below).

Needle File

Five inches in length and thinner than a pencil, needle files are available at jewelry supply shops. Get a flat file with a tapered point and a round file, as pictured below. (*See* Flush-Cutting on page 34 for more detail on this tool's usage.)

Frisbees

Available at your local sporting goods store, these plastic discs are ideal for holding jump rings during chain construction. Notice that I have separated the red disc into thirds with duct tape to sort and contain different sizes of jump rings. In a pinch or on the go, you can place one frisbee over the other and duct-tape the seam to hold your jump rings, chains, and tools.

Nalgene bottle

Available at your local camping store, these 8-inch-tall durable bottles not only hold your favorite beverage, but also make a handy holder to carry duct tape when making separations on disks (*see* illustration at right).

Medical Vials

Medical vials are available at medical supply stores or online. These durable plastic tubes (those pictured below are manufactured by Sarstedt) are perfect for storing jump rings, beads, and clasps.

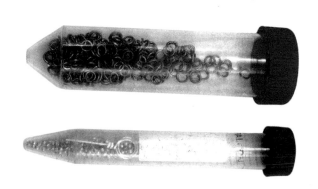

Pliers

There are many types of pliers to choose from, with differently shaped jaws, spring actions, overall lengths, and handle grip ergonomics. Try to think of pliers as extensions of your hands and fingers when handcrafting chains. Because of my large hands, I use 6-inch pliers so that the handle ends do not press into the center of my palm. (I use the Swanstrom brand.) While cheaper tools will work fine to get started, I recommend getting the best you can afford and taking good care of them. It will make a difference in the quality of your chain.

Flat-Nose Pliers

You will need two pairs of flat-nose pliers, one for each hand to work in tandem. This tool is 6 inches in length, with jaws that taper to rectangular tips. The tips' width should measure ¼ inch or 6mm to hold enough surface area on a 18-gauge ring with a paper-thin thickness. Available at jewelry supply shops, the pliers should be smooth-jawed, with no teeth where the pliers meet the soft metal wire.

Chain-Nose Pliers

You will need two chain-nose pliers, one for each hand to work in tandem. This tool is 6 inches in length, with jaws that taper to a half-round point. They are useful for getting into tight spaces in the chain, setting beads, and smashing crimp beads. Available at jewelry supply shops, the pliers should be smooth-jawed, with no teeth. Needle-nose pliers may be used as a substitute; their jaws taper to a fine point.

Round-Nose Pliers

You will need only one pair of round-nose pliers. They are 6 inches in overall length, with jaws that taper to a blunt point, and are available at jewelry supply shops. Check that the jaws are round and not oval. This tool is essential for making the Rosary design (*see* page 62), the Spade design (*see* page 68), and for making the forged S-clasp and earring backings (*see* pages 36–41).

Wire

Wire is sold commercially in a variety of shapes: square, triangular, rectangular, oval, and half-round. All of the chain designs in this book use round wire. Wire is shaped by a process called *wire drawing*, in which the wire is pulled through a drawplate, making the wire thinner, stronger, and causing it to conform to the shape of the hole within the plate. New wire is soft on account of a process called *annealing*, which reduces stress in a metal by heating the wire and then allowing it to cool slowly.

You can purchase wire at different stages of annealation. Half-hard or medium wire has been annealed halfway and is the standard for most jewelry wire. I do not recommend hard wire, because as you wrap the wire around the mandrel into coils, you are quadrupling the wire's physical tensile strength by "work hardening" the wire.

As I mentioned in the last chapter, round wire is typically measured and sold in diameter increments, called gauges in the United States. The gauge number increases as the wire diameter decreases. Therefore, 18-gauge wire is thinner than 14-gauge. In Canada and Europe, round wire is measured and sold in quarter-millimeter increments.

Pictured below is a collage of different wires. The large white loop is 18-gauge sterling silver wire. The black plastic spools are finer 22- and 24-gauge silver wire. The white spools are brass and NuGold wire. The large black-and-white loop is plastic-coated 14-gauge electrical copper wire that I salvaged from a local electrician.

Metals

The jewelry designs selected for this book were crafted from a range of metal alloy round wire. Alloys are a combination of two or more metals that have been smelted together to create an improved substance. For example, sterling silver is more malleable than pure silver, gold alloy is cheaper than pure gold, and brass alloy is stronger than either of its components.

Sterling Silver

Pure metals are too soft for chain making; that is why we use a composition of metals that are smelted together into an alloy. Sterling silver is one such alloy, which combines 92.5% pure silver with 7.5% copper. This composition has been especially designed to allow the metal to be malleable for blacksmithing with a hammer and anvil. I have a personal affinity for sterling silver and use it for my artwork on account of its color, shine, strength, malleability, and affordability. Sterling silver round wire is typically sold by the troy ounce (toz) on a price break system; the more you buy, the cheaper it is per troy ounce.

Copper

I highly recommend that you practice your chain-making skills with an inexpensive base metal wire like copper before you move on to sterling silver or gold. I do my research and development work in copper because it is inexpensive, readily available, and has physical characteristics similar to those of sterling silver. You can find small spools of 18-gauge copper round wire at your local hardware store. Look in the electrical wiring section to find 14-gauge copper round wire, sold by the foot. If you cannot find raw wire, you might have to strip the plastic insulation off 14-gauge electrical copper wire.

Nickel Silver

Also known as German Silver and White Brass, this composition of 60% copper, 20% nickel, and 20% zinc creates an inexpensive and strong wire. It is similar to sterling silver in color, yet it does not hold a shine, degrading to a matte finish similar to that of an American nickel coin.

Plastic-coated Copper

Readily found in most craft stores, plastic-coated wire is 18-gauge copper wire with a thin plastic-colored coating to prevent tarnishing. If you choose this colorful option, keep in mind that this coating also gives the wire a larger diameter, which means you will need to wrap it around a larger mandrel in order to make the Byzantine chain.

Gold

Gold is purchased in different karat (k) values that indicate its alloy composition. A karat number signifies the relative amount of gold in an alloy. For example, 24k gold is 100% pure gold, 18k gold is 75% gold, 12k gold is 50% gold, and 6k gold is only 25% gold. Pure gold is too soft for making chain, so it is smelted with silver and copper to achieve a desired alloy. Each alloy produces a color indicative of its ingredients. Yellow gold is an alloy of gold, silver, and copper; white gold is an alloy of gold and silver; and rose gold is an alloy of gold and copper. The strongest gold alloy is 12k yellow gold, which combines 50% gold, 25% silver, and 25% copper. Gold wire is sold by the pennyweight (dwt); twenty pennyweights equal one troy ounce (toz). When considering gold wire, keep in mind that the cost is quite prohibitive, being forty to fifty times more expensive than sterling silver. Several cost-effective alternatives are available, such as gold-filled wire and NuGold wire.

Gold-filled

Gold-filled is a misnomer; more accurately it's known as rolled gold or gold overlay. A typical alloy is labeled 14/20 GF, which indicates that 1/20 of the wire's weight ratio is a thin layer of 14k gold that is heat- and pressure-bonded to the outside of a cheaper metal base, such as copper or brass. Since the base metal is sealed within the bonded gold, it cannot leach out and tarnish the wire. However, precautions must be taken not to scratch through the soft gold surface. If you want the look of gold without the huge cost, this option is ideal.

NuGold

NuGold is an alloy composed of smelting 85% copper with 15% zinc. It is also known as Low Brass, Red Brass, Jeweler's Bronze, Pinchbeck, Dixgold, and Merlin's Gold. NuGold is relatively inexpensive and available through retailers (*see* Resources on page 126).

Brass

Brass is a family of alloys composed by smelting copper and zinc together into a yellow metal that is stronger than either of its separate components. Bright yellow "brassy" colored brass, also known as High Brass, is achieved by smelting 70% copper with 30% zinc.

> ### IF YOU ARE CONSIDERING ALUMINUM...
> *Aluminum is an inexpensive, silvery-white metal with little shine. While spools of aluminum wire are readily available, this wire is too soft for chain making. However, there are endless variations of alloys available in the industry, and finding an alloy of aluminum with the right mixture of strength and flexibility is conceivable.*

Bead-Setting Tools

Although each of the sixteen chain designs in this book can stand alone, the addition of beads changes the jewelry's content by adding complementary colors, visual depth, texture, and physical mass. The beading embellishment technique involves intermittently weaving a length of beading wire through predrilled beads in the chain design. The beaded wire is then secured at both ends with a crimp bead that is smashed over the beading wire. The beauty of this beading technique is that it works in harmony with the Byzantine chain designs and allows the addition of beads without limiting the overall flexibility of the chain. In addition, by using beading wire, the beads are not static, as they would be in a bezel setting, but are instead allowed to spin freely along the drilled axis. The amazing advantages of this technique, besides allowing flexibility and axis movement, are its strength and resistance to wear.

Beading Wire

Available at jewelry supply shops, this multi-stranded nylon-coated stainless steel wire is used to attach beads to jewelry. The strand-count and diameter of beading wire indicates its linear strength. There is a wide variety of strand-count diameter thicknesses and finish colors of beading wire available. I use the 49-strand, 0.013 inch (0.33mm) diameter, with a clear/gray finish, in a 30-foot spool.

Bead Reamer

Available at jewelry supply stores, these fine-pointed diamond-plated bits taper from a 2mm diameter down to a fine point. A bead reamer is used with an electric screwdriver to slowly enlarge the predrilled hole within gemstones to allow 18-gauge ingress. (*See* Bead Reaming on page 63 for more details on using this tool.)

Crimp Beads

Available at jewelry supply shops, these tiny millimeter-length tubes are utilized in tandem with beading wire to set gemstone beads. Crimp beads are sold in a wide variety of metals, tube lengths, and inside diameter hole sizes. I use sterling silver crimp beads that are 1mm in diameter with an inside diameter hole of 0.030 inch (0.76mm). Notice that the inside diameter is two times larger than the beading wire's diameter, which allows just enough room for the beading wire to pass through the crimp bead twice and hold securely when smashed. The proper size of the crimping bead is crucial to securing the embellishment. The inside diameter hole size of the crimp bead should be greater than double, but less than three times, the beading wire's diameter.

Beads

Gemstone is a collective name for all ornamental stone materials found on the Earth's crust. A mind-numbing assortment of gemstone beads are available at bead shops, craft stores, and through catalogue companies (*see* Resources on page 126). Beads are typically sold by even-numbered millimeter diameters that are predrilled on 15-inch bead strand lengths. I recommend getting an assortment of sizes. I use 2, 3, 4, 6, and 8mm round beads in the chain designs in this book. Below are a few of my favorite gemstones:

 **Amethyst**–Translucent purple quartz, worn as an amulet against drunkenness; represents Pisces on the Zodiac and the month of February.

 **Lapis Lazuli**–Opaque blue rock with flecks of gold-colored pyrite and white calcite; worn to ease eye troubles; represents the planet Jupiter.

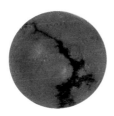 **Turquoise**–Opaque blue to green mineral with a waxy luster and black matrix veins; represents Aquarius on the Zodiac and the month of December.

 **Carnelian**–Translucent red-orange quartz; protects against the evil eye and is given as a token on fifth wedding anniversaries.

 **Jade**–Green, white, black, and red opaque mineral with a waxy luster; worn as protection from lightning and to heal the kidneys.

 **Hematite**–Opaque gray-black mineral with a metallic sheen; naturally found with red iron stripes; worn to balance energies.

 **Moss Agate**–Translucent quartz with green hornblende in mosslike patterns; worn by farmers to ensure a good harvest.

 **Onyx**–Opaque mineral naturally banded with white; typically dyed black, red, blue, or green; used to carve cameo relief images.

 **Malachite**–Opaque green mineral with lighter bands and a silky luster; worn to ease child labor and protect infants and children.

Do not be led to believe that beads have to be round or made of stone. The only prerequisite is that the bead have a drilled hole in order to be threaded with beading wire. You can buy predrilled beads in a wide variety of shapes: oval, teardrop, hourglass, pebble, donut, abacus, twist, barrel, cone, tube, diamond, star, heart, cube, faceted, triangular, rectangular, tetrahedron, and dodecahedron—there are even square ones with letters on them. Below are some of my favorite alternatives:

Metal–Available in a wide variety of shapes and types. Pictured is a laser-etched sterling silver bead that sparkles in the light.

Glass–Manufactured beads are available in every color imaginable. Pictured is a handmade bead from Venice, Italy.

Pearl–Created inside a mussel shell, pearl beads are available in a range of shapes, sizes, colors, and lusters. Pictured is a potato pearl.

Metal Clay–This modern marvel can be formed by hand and fired to hardness in your kiln. This charm was made by artist Sherri Haab.

Wood–Lathed into shape, wooden beads typically are carved with symbols or painted. Sandalwood beads, like the one pictured, are lightweight and smell great.

Amber–Amber is translucent fossilized tree resin and organic matter that is millions of years old. It is typically yellow-gold with air bubbles.

Wire Skills

This section will take you step by step through the chain-making process, from wrapping wire into coils to jump-ring cutting techniques, and concludes with ways to evaluate the chain's flexibility. For the completion of a chain, we will go through hand-forging S-clasps and making earring backings.

Hand Wrapping

Hand wrapping invloves wrapping metal wire around a mandrel to create a linear coil in which to cut off jump rings. This ensures that each jump ring will have an identical diameter, which is essential for even flexibility in the chain. Wrapping wire requires hand-eye coordination to guide the wire in a continuous coil without introducing any gaps or overlapping the wire. To gain this coordination, I strongly recommend that you wrap a few inches of wire by hand before attempting the Power Wrapping technique on pages 30–31. Although hand wrapping is slow and laborious, it will strengthen your hands, reduce carpal-tunnel fatigue, and give you a strong handshake!

Start with a wrapping mandrel that is the correct size for the wire you're wrapping, an 18-inch length of round wire, and a cloth bandanna.

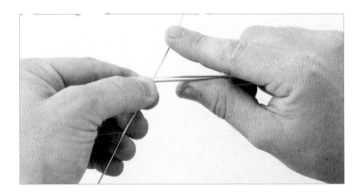

1. Holding the mandrel horizontally in your left hand, add the length of wire with your right hand, leaving a 3-inch tail hanging down.

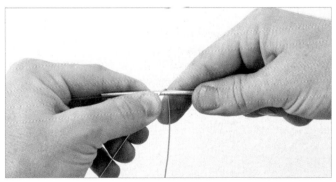

2. Push the wire over the mandrel with your index finger.

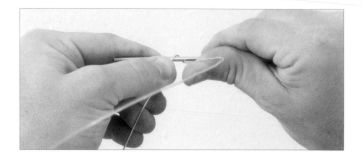

3. After the index finger has pushed the wire down, hook your thumb behind the wire and push it up, making a smooth transition in order to maintain the coil's spring tension.

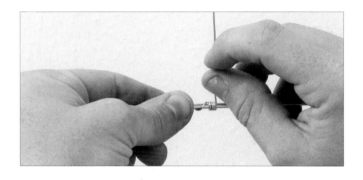

4. After the thumb has pulled the wire up, move the index finger over the thumb and push the wire down, maintaining the coil's spring tension with a smooth transition.

5. Pull the wire up with your thumb, so that the wire is wrapping clockwise around the mandrel. The length of wire will flip past your face; be careful that the wire point does not poke you.

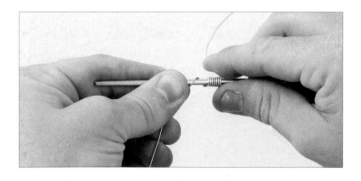

6. Apply your finger's pressure to the straight wire within an inch of where it is being bent around the mandrel into a coil.

Note: The physical action of wrapping quadruples the tensile strength of the wire, creating a strong unsoldered chain.

7. After six to ten coils, you will feel the coil's spring tension shorten the 3-inch tail. Although the tail length is designed to shorten as the coil grows, an inch or two must be maintained in order to counter the spring tension from the wrapping action. To assist holding the tail's spring tension, place a folded bandanna around the mandrel and tail.

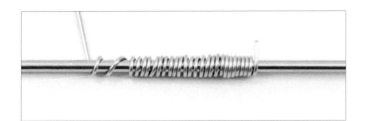

It is common for the first few wraps to have gaps when hand wrapping. As the coil lengthens, concentrate on feeding the wire onto the coil so that each wrap lies directly next to the previous wrap without any gaps.

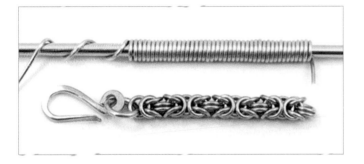

8. Take caution when you reach the end of the wire, as the spring tension can cause the end tip to spin backward through your fingers, possibly cutting you.

The length of the wrapped coil will equal the length of the Byzantine chain you are creating. Pictured on the left is an 18-gauge brass round wire that was wrapped onto a 3.25mm mandrel, creating a 4.5cm length coil that can be cut into 45 jump rings. This made a 4.5cm Byzantine chain. Notice the correlation between the wire thickness (1.02mm) times the number of loops in coil (45) and the coil's length (4.5cm), producing a predictable number of jump rings (45).

Precut Jump Rings

Commercially available jump rings are typically sold in outside diameters. To determine the outside diameter you will need, measure the wire gauge in millimeters, multiply by 3.14, which yields the inside diameter, and then add two times the wire thickness for the outside diameter. To this number add a ¼ millimeter to compensate for the mass-produced cutting technique. (Commercial jump rings are cut with a separating disk, which removes a portion of the jump ring's diameter.)

For example, an 18-gauge wire, 1.02mm thick, multiplied by 3.14 yields an approximate inside diameter of 3.25mm. Add two times the wire thickness (1.02mm) to yield an outside diameter of 5.25mm. Add .25mm to obtain the outside diameter needed to purchase your jump rings. In this example you would need jump rings with a 5.5mm diameter.

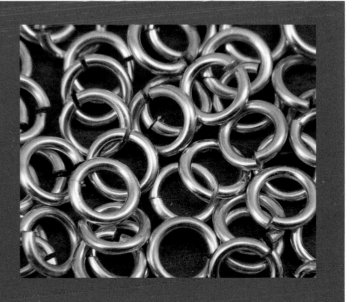

Power Wrapping

For years I used a carpenter's hand drill to wrap wire quickly, but recently I traded up to an electric screwdriver because of its ease of use and availability. Let me clarify that this is a cordless screwdriver that runs on a 3.6-volt battery, not a cordless drill that runs on an 18-volt battery. Do not attempt to wrap wire with any type of drill; they have much more speed and torque than is required and can be quite dangerous. Power wrapping is significantly faster and creates a more consistent coil; however, this speed can be detrimental if you have not mastered the rudimentary function of hand wrapping wire (*see* pages 27–29).

Start with a knitting needle (used as a mandrel) that is the correct size for the wire you are wrapping; a length of round wire; and a fully charged electric screwdriver with a chuck adaptor. You may need to clip off the pointed tip of the knitting needle so that it will fit securely in the chuck.

1. With the mandrel centered between the three prongs, tighten the chuck. Insert the end of the wire between two of the three prongs. This will hold the spring tension.

2. Bend the wire at a right angle where it exits the chuck so that the wire is perpendicular to the mandrel.

3. Hold the wire in the knuckles of one hand and steady it with your thumb. Press and release the power button in the forward position so that the wire wraps clockwise.

4. Support the wire and mandrel with your index finger and thumb as it feeds onto the mandrel.

A subtle dexterity is required to control the angle at which the wire feeds into the coil. If the wire is angled slightly inward toward the coil, it will overlap the previous wire on top of the coil. If the wire is angled slightly outward and away from the coil, it will create gaps between each coil.

5. Press and release the power button to allow the mandrel to spin a few times and then stop. You will need to continually reposition your hand in order to feed the wire onto the coil correctly as it gradually increases in length.

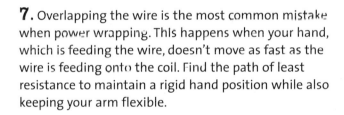

6. If you feel friction from the wire as it is pulled though your hand, try holding the wire with a bandanna, but do not let the cloth get pulled into the wire wrapping.

7. Overlapping the wire is the most common mistake when power wrapping. This happens when your hand, which is feeding the wire, doesn't move as fast as the wire is feeding onto the coil. Find the path of least resistance to maintain a rigid hand position while also keeping your arm flexible.

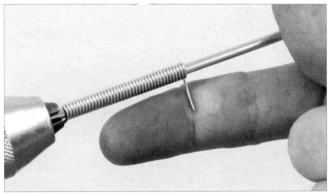

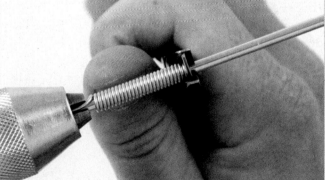

8. STOP! when you feel the end of the wire being pulled through your hand. The spring tension has increased with the coil's length, and if the wire spins backward through your fingers, it will definitely cut you!

9. Use flat-nose pliers to finish wrapping the tip of the wire into the coil.

Burr-Cutting

When cutting jump rings, keep in mind that speed is no substitute for consistency and quality, which will be evident in the chain's finish. Cutting jump rings requires dexterity to maintain a consistent cutting position of the cutter's blades and the coil, as well as hand-eye coordination to control the depth of each cut. If the laborious chore of cutting your own jump rings is not your style, you can simply buy pre-cut jump rings (*see* Precut Jump Rings on page 29).

Start with side cutters; several wrapped coils; and a handkerchief spread across your lap to catch the jump rings.

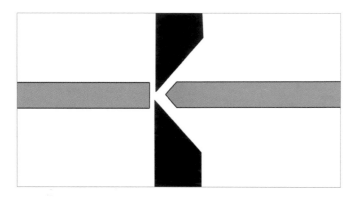

This diagram shows a horizontal piece of wire being cut by side cutters. Notice that the blades are wedge-shaped; one side is flat, which leaves the wire flush, while the other side is angled, which cuts the wire with a pointed burr. This burr is created from the serrating action of the side cutter's blades. As the blades pinch into the wire, the wire must stretch until it snaps off.

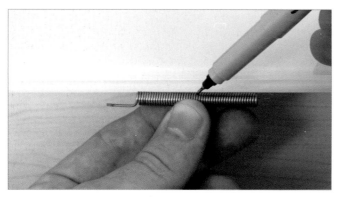

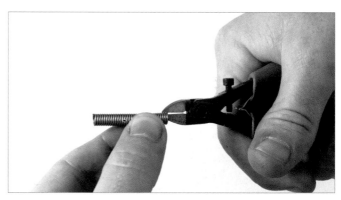

1. Hold the coil parallel to a straight edge and draw a line (cut line) along the coil's length with a marker. You will follow this line to cut the coil into jump rings.

2. Hold the coil between your thumb and index finger, with the cut line centered and facing upward. Cut off the wrapping tail.

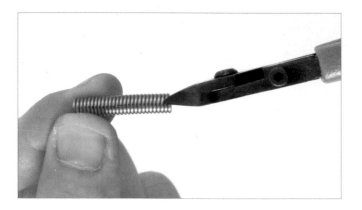

Notice that the handles of the side cutters are not in line with the blades. To compensate for this difference, always line up the flat side of the blades with the cut line—not the pliers' handles. This is key to ensuring that the flat side of the blade is cutting through the wire perpendicularly.

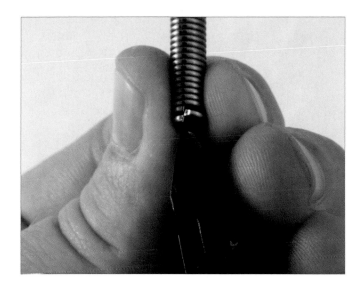

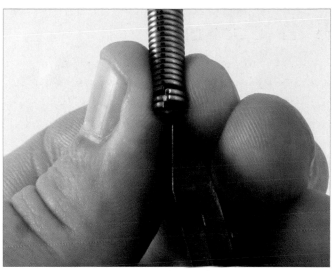

3. Start by cutting off one jump ring at a time. Control the depth of the blades to cut through one wire thickness (cutting halfway through the wire will produce a sharp gargoyle head; *see* below).

4. Advance to cutting off two jump rings at a time. Again, allow the depth of the blades to cut through both wires without nicking the third wire.

Burr-Cutting: Quality Control

When you have a pile of cut jump rings, spread them out on a contrasting colored surface so that the rings stand out. Look for nicked, lopsided, oval, gapped, or oddly shaped jump rings; separate and recycle them. With practice, ninety-nine percent of your jump rings will turn out perfectly, yet you should always keep a keen eye for the occasional odd ring. This dedication to quality control will be evident in the equally spaced finish and smooth feel of your chain.

Jump rings can be inferior or below standard for a variety of reasons. The top left ring is ideal. It is perfectly round and makes a full circumference. The top right ring has a gargoyle head, which is caused by cutting halfway through the wire, leaving a sharp burr. The ring below left is lopsided due to either dull cutting blades or overlapping wire. The ring below right is gapped, which is caused by cutting short of a full circumference, making an oval ring of a smaller inside diameter than the ideal derived from the Pi ratio (*see* pages 10–11).

Flush-Cutting

Flush-cutting extends the previous cutting technique to eliminate the burr. It requires two cuts per jump ring: the first to remove the burr and the second to cut the jump ring off the coil. I use this technique for cutting 14-gauge jump rings, which are only used as single accent rings where the burr is more noticeable and distracting to the eye. While flush-cutting and proper filing will produce visually seamless rings, keep in mind that the rings will be slightly smaller than their wrapped diameter.

Start with side cutters; a 14-gauge coil; and a handkerchief spread across your lap to catch the jump rings.

1. With the flat side of the side cutters facing right, cut off the wrapping tail, leaving the end of the coil with a burr.

2. Turn the side cutters 180 degrees so that the flat side is facing left. Place the tips of the blades just to the left of the burr, with only enough depth to cut through one wire. Cut off the burr, creating a double-sided burr and leaving the end of the coil flush.

As flush-cutting produces rings with a slightly smaller diameter, you will not be able to make the 14-gauge Byzantine chain from these rings. If you wish to challenge your sanity by making the Byzantine chain with flush-cut jump rings, you must compensate for this diameter shrinkage by wrapping the wire around a mandrel that is a quarter millimeter larger in diameter than the size determined by the Pi ratio (see pages 10–11).

3. Turn the side cutter 180 degrees so that the flat side is facing right. Place the cutter's tips just at the previously cut flush end, with depth enough to cut through one wire. Cut off the flush jump ring, leaving the end of the coil with a burr. Continue steps 2 and 3, repeatedly turning the cutters back and forth between each cut, sequentially cutting off a double-sided burr or a flush-cut jump ring.

4. Because of the slight gap, close each jump ring with equal pressure from each pair of flat-nose pliers by using a twisting action and gently pushing the tips together. As you look at the wire's profile, make sure it is flat and that neither the front nor back edges of the cut protrude forward or backward.

5. As you look at the ring's profile, it should also be circular. Neither the top nor the bottom edges of the cut should protrude up or down, which will be evident when you begin to file—as the file will not mark what it cannot touch.

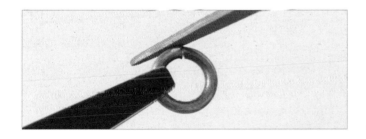

6. Hold the flat file gingerly with your right hand's fingertips, supported by the thumb. Be gentle with the file, as it will remove the soft metal rapidly. Push the file over the top of the jump ring's joint, removing any metal burrage.

7. Use a round file inside the ring to round out the bottom of the jump ring's joint, removing any metal burrage.

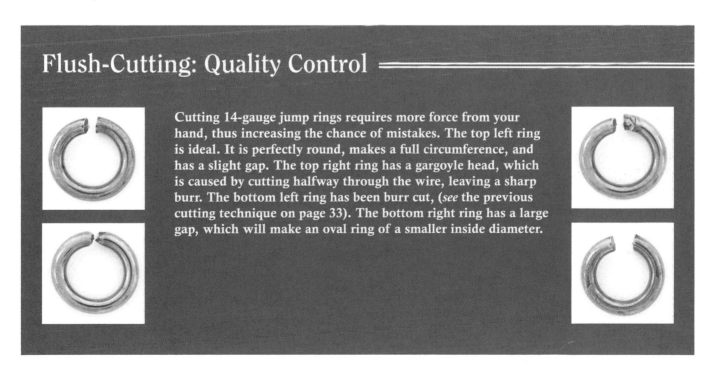

Flush-Cutting: Quality Control

Cutting 14-gauge jump rings requires more force from your hand, thus increasing the chance of mistakes. The top left ring is ideal. It is perfectly round, makes a full circumference, and has a slight gap. The top right ring has a gargoyle head, which is caused by cutting halfway through the wire, leaving a sharp burr. The bottom left ring has been burr cut, (*see* the previous cutting technique on page 33). The bottom right ring has a large gap, which will make an oval ring of a smaller inside diameter.

Forging Clasps

A clasp securely connects a length of chain and allows the wearer to put on or take off the piece of jewelry. Typically, this is accomplished by placing a hook on one end and a catch ring on the other. In my opinion, however, the majority of available clasps are physically flawed, with tiny spring-action moving parts that break and which are aesthetically inadequate to complete my chain designs.

After searching in vain for a better clasp, I designed my own 14-gauge sterling silver S-clasp on paper and then sculpted it with a hammer and anvil. By intuitive design, its profile exhibits an uncanny similarity to the capital letter S when I sign my name. This clasp and three catch rings measure 1½ inches in combined length.

The size and length of the round wire you use will determine the size of the S-clasp you will create. As the length increases, so must the diameters of the top and bottom loops.

A catch ring is used with a clasp to connect the chain. I typically finish a chain with twin catch rings, adding two 14-gauge jump rings, assembled 1+1. This sequence provides the wearer with a chain length adjustability of ¼ inch and complements the clasp symmetrically.

An S-clasp and catch rings secure a length of chain, measuring 1½ inches in combined length.

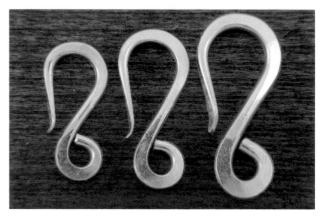

Pictured above, a small 14-gauge S-clasp at 4cm; a medium 14-gauge at 4.5cm; and a large 12-gauge at 5.0cm.

Two 14-gauge jump rings are used as twin catch rings to finish a chain, which will allow the chain to connect to the S-clasp.

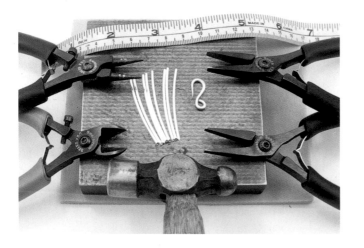

Start with an anvil; hammer; round-nose pliers; flat-nose pliers; side cutters; flat file; measuring tape; and 14-gauge wire.

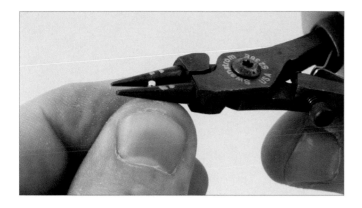

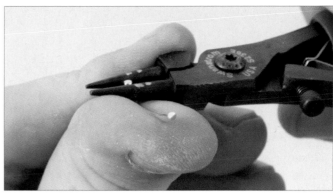

1. Cut the 14-gauge wire into several 4cm sections. Notice that one end has a burr while the other end is flat. Grab the flat end of the wire section with the round-nose pliers and position the wire halfway (3mm) into the jaws.

2. Bend the wire toward you around the jaw of the pliers with your thumb by applying pressure where the wire is bending, rotating the pliers against the bend and equalizing pressure.

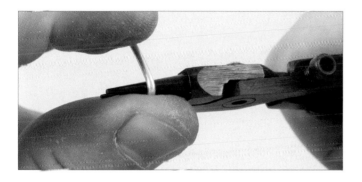

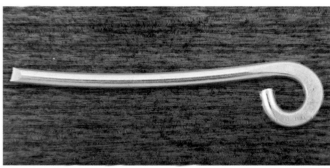

3. Complete the loop with your index finger, pushing the wire over the round jaw while rotating the pliers.

4. Hold the wire with the small loop toward you on the anvil, and gently hammer the loop until it flattens slightly. Apply force in a series of small taps, as the metal is quite malleable.

5. Notice that as you flattened the loop it stretches out, creating a gap where the loop meets the wire. Close this gap by holding the loop flat against the anvil and pressing the loop closed with the jaw tips of flat-nose pliers.

6. Tighten the loop by gently pressing the wire's tip down, creating a smooth spiral appearance. For faster assembly and in order to gain a better feel for this technique, I recommend making several clasps at a time.

In order to maintain an equilateral flattening of the round wire as it is pulled into the tongue shape, the flat side of the hammer's head must be horizontal to the anvil when it strikes the wire or the tongue will get pulled asymmetrically.

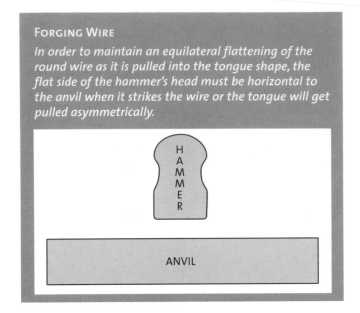

7. Forge the tongue of the clasp from a third to slightly less than half of the remaining round wire, leaving plenty of unhammered round wire for bending the large loop later.

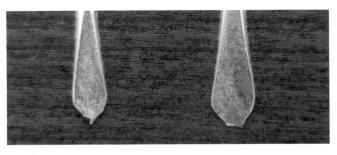

8. Hold the small loop perpendicular to the anvil with the burr-tipped wire toward you. In a series of small taps, hammer the wire into a flattened tongue shape.

9. Finish the tongue by directing more force at the tip in order to flare it out to roughly twice the width of the original wire. If the small loop is facing upward, the hammer-marked tongue will be on the outside of the finished clasp. If the small loop is facing downward, the smooth anvil side will be on the outside of the clasp.

10. Use a flat file to smooth and round the tongue's profile, but do not sharpen the tip. A few gentle strokes are sufficient. Finish smoothing with a 3m sanding pad.

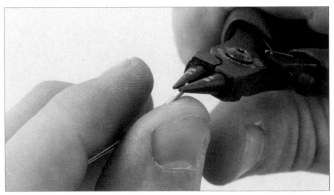

11. Place the tip of the tongue halfway into the jaws of the round-nose pliers and give a slight 45-degree bend toward the loop. This slight bend, or "ski tip," serves as the catch ring gateway.

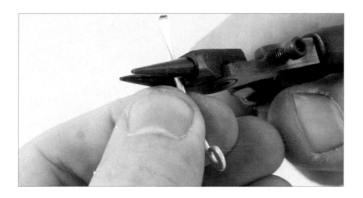

12. Position the wire at the back end of the jaws of the round-nose pliers, about 5mm, and grab the wire halfway between the ski tip and the loop.

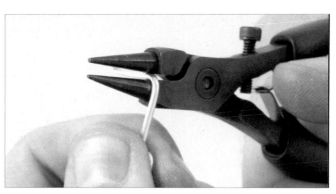

13. Pull the loop and ski tip toward each other until they are parallel to each other.

14. At this point you want to evaluate whether to bring the loop closer to the ski tip or vice versa. Ultimately, the bottom of the ski tip should meet the loop to create a gateway for the catch ring to pass through.

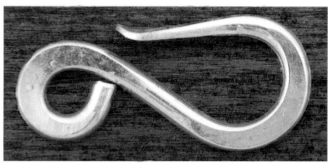

15. Hold the small loop parallel to the anvil in your left hand, with the large loop toward you. Gently hammer the remaining round wire, leaving the wire thicker toward both the small loop and the top of the tongue, and thinner between the two. Be careful not to hit the tongue in this operation or, more importantly, your fingers.

16. You also may need to straighten the clasp. Line up the small loop with the large loop, and center the ski tip over the small loop. Make sure that the tongue is perpendicular to both loops.

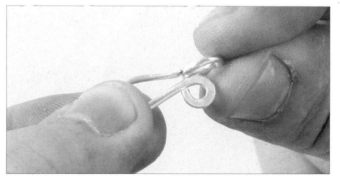

17. Upon completing the S-clasp, you should evaluate its shape and adjust its spring tension. By forging the large loop, a spring is created at the gateway between the bottom of the ski tip and the small loop; adjust this gateway to allow a 14-gauge catch ring to pass through with slight resistance.

Earring Backs

An earring back suspends an earring design from a small loop that is connected to a larger hoop. The back travels through the earlobe and counterbalances the design's weight with the length of wire behind the earlobe. The earring backs below are crafted from round wire using a few simple hand tools and techniques borrowed from forging clasps (*see* pages 36–39). Handcrafted earring backs add a special beauty compared with the sterile look of those that are manufactured. Since I do not wear earrings, I don't have any opinions about what their proper shape, weight, and fit should be. However, every woman I've made earrings for seems to have had a different view. The beauty of crafting your own earring backs is that you can customize them in a variety of shapes and sizes. High-karat gold or surgical steel are the best choice for those people who are sensitive or allergic to base metals.

Start with flat-nose and round-nose pliers; hammer; anvil; needle file; bandanna; and 20 inches of 18-gauge wire.

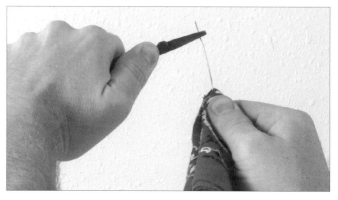

1. Cut a 20-inch length of 18-gauge wire. While holding the wire in your flat-nose pliers, pull it through a folded bandanna. This will increase the wire's tensile strength and straighten out any kinks in the wire. Cut the wire into ten 2-inch lengths.

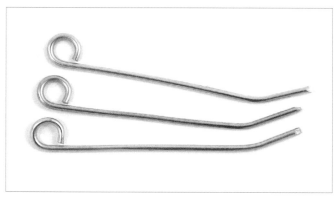

2. Wrap a small loop with a 3mm diameter at one end. Hold the wire with the round-nose pliers ¼ inch from the end. Bend the wire upward at a 45-degree angle.

3. Bend the center of the wire around a 7mm mandrel. (In this photo, I'm using a cheap mechanical pencil.) Bend the end with the small loop around the mandrel and over the large hoop, with the bent tail sticking out.

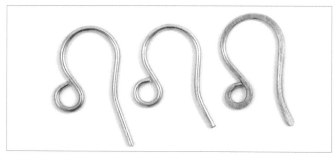

4. The earring back on the left has a long tail to counterbalance a long earring. The back's tail in the middle has been trimmed for a short earring. The back on the right has been hammered—notice how the shape changes with forging.

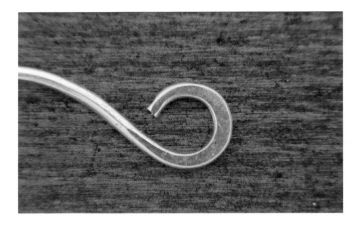

5. With the hammer and anvil, gently tap the small loop. This will cause the loop to spread open.

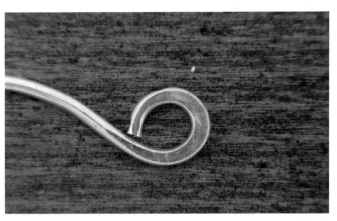

6. Use the flat-nose pliers to squeeze the small loop closed.

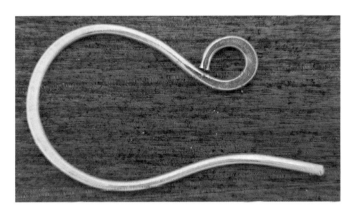

7. Forge the top of the large hoop to add strength to the earring back, as well as a thinner profile for earlobe comfort.

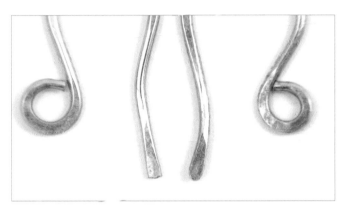

8. Finish the back by forging the tip slightly. Then file the tip smooth and round, to facilitate easier earlobe ingress. Use 3m sanding pads for smoothing.

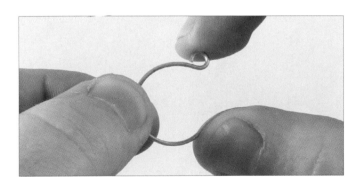

9. Gently adjust the curvature of the large loop by pulling the small loop toward the S-curving tail.

10. Use both pairs of flat-nosed pliers to twist open the small loop. Add the earring design onto the backing.

Byzantine Components

This section illustrates step by step the assembly of the double, Inca puño, and Byzantine chains. We will explore the fundamentals of the three chain patterns as well as the relationship of the double and Inca puño chains to the Byzantine chain.

The Byzantine chain is a sequential chain pattern that can be broken down into two basic building blocks: the knot formation of the Inca puño chain and the connector pair of the double chain. By alternating these two chain concepts, a new and completely different design—the Byzantine chain—is assembled. The Byzantine chain is based on assembling six jump rings in a 2+2+2 pattern. Two rings serve as the connector pair, and four rings comprise the knot formation. After assembling each set of six jump rings, the knot formation is folded back and angled open to create a rectangular opening in which to add the next 2+2+2 pattern. The unique sequential design of the Byzantine chain allows for the addition of crown formations, which are the genesis of the designs in this book.

Knot Formations

The connector pairs (the blue and gray rings in the illustration at the right) secure the folded-back and opened knot formations (the red and green rings) on both sides.

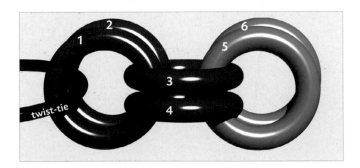

1. This sequence of six jump rings, assembled 2+2+2, is referred to as the *open knot sequence*. The term "open knot" refers to the red pair of rings 3 and 4 and the green pair of rings 5 and 6.

2. This image illustrates the *knot formation*. After the green pair of rings 5 and 6 has been folded back and the red pair of rings 3 and 4 has been angled open to reveal a rectangular opening, the next pair of jump rings will be added to continue the Byzantine chain.

The Connector Pair

Connector pairs (blue and gray rings on the previous page) secure the knot formations on both sides. Thus, the chain begins and ends with a connector pair, which allows room to add a larger 14-gauge ring for the clasp and catch ring. The two rings in the connector pair always remain parallel to each another. These rings enable you to splice two lengths of chain together, or shorten a chain, as seen below.

1. Both ends of the chain must be in the open knot sequence. Fold back and angle open one knot formation, and add a single jump ring through the rectangular opening.

2. Fold back and angle open the second knot, and add the single jump ring through the second knot's rectangular opening.

3. Close this first jump ring with chain-nose pliers. Add a second jump ring parallel to the previous jump ring. This ring is difficult to close due to the tight space between the knot formations. Squeeze the ring's tips together.

4. Close this second jump ring with chain-nose pliers.

Double Chain

The double chain is based on assembling two jump rings in a 2+2+2+2 continuous pattern, with each pair of two rings acting as a connector pair. Since this chain is a repeating design without any knot formations, each jump ring must be slightly smaller in diameter to compensate for the lack of knot formations. The simplicity of this chain design can offset a complex centerpiece.

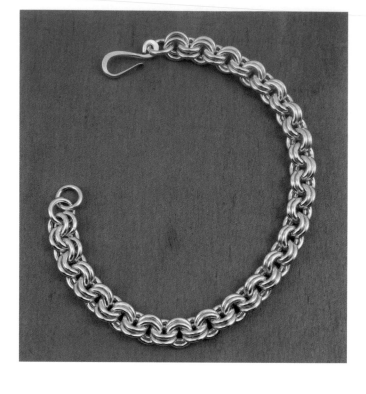

This 9-inch 14-gauge sterling silver double chain is a simple yet masculine bracelet, complete with a large 12-gauge S-clasp.

1. Add two jump rings (shown in blue) onto the twist tie. Add two more jump rings (show in gray) to rings 1 and 2.

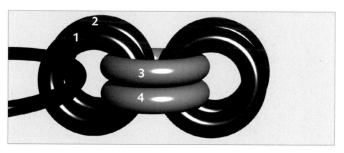

2. Add two jump rings to rings 3 and 4.

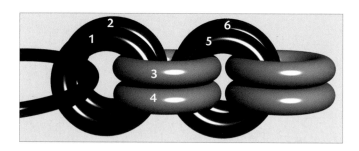

3. Add two jump rings to rings 5 and 6.

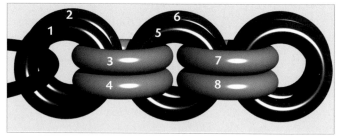

4. Add two jump rings to 7 and 8.

Inca Puño Chain

The Inca puño chain is based on assembling four jump rings into a 2+2 pattern. These four rings comprise the knot formation, which is folded back and angled open to create a rectangular opening for the next 2+2 pattern. This chain has a distinctive repeating design without any connector pairs between the knots. Thus, each jump ring must be slightly larger in diameter to allow the knot to fold back into the previous knot. Note that four Byzantine-size jump rings are used for the two sets of connector pairs. These are used at the beginning and the end of the chain to hold the end knot formation open, give closure to the chain, and allow room to add the larger 14-gauge rings that hold the clasp and catch ring.

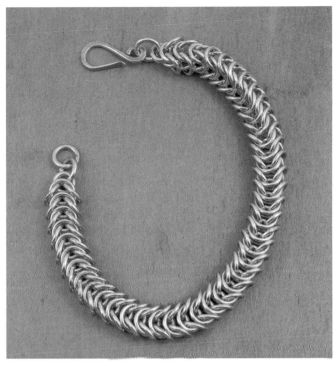

The Inca puño bracelet pictured above was crafted from 14-gauge recycled electrical copper wire. Measuring 9 inches with a large 12-gauge S-clasp, this hefty piece weighs over 2 ounces.

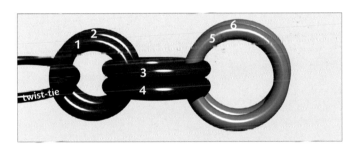

1. Add two Byzantine-sized jump rings (shown in blue above) to the black twist tie to serve as the connector pair. Add four, assembled 2+2, Inca puño–sized jump rings (shown in red and green).

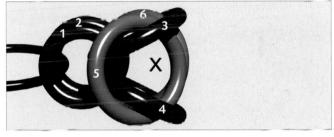

2. Fold back green rings 5 and 6 and open red rings 3 and 4 to create the rectangular opening, marked with an X above.

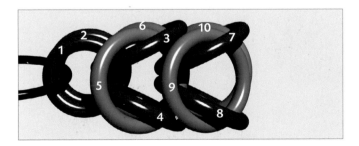

3. Add four rings, assembled 2+2, onto the previous knot. Fold back the green rings 9 and 10 and open red rings 7 and 8 to create the rectangular opening.

4. Add four rings, assembled 2+2, onto the previous knot. Repeat step 3 until you reach your desired chain length.

Byzantine Chain

Throughout the length of the chain-making process, a sequential pattern is created as the knot formations reverse to mirror one another in harmony with the 90-degree turning of the connector pairs. As the knot formations are folded back and angled open, a rectangular opening is created for the next connector pair. Thus, the connector pair secures the folded-back open position of the knot formation on both sides.

This 8-inch Byzantine bracelet was crafted from 14-gauge yellow brass wire, complete with a large 12-gauge S-clasp.

1. The illustration above shows the Byzantine chain separated into its two components: the connector pairs (blue and gray) and the knot formations (red and green).

2. Add six jump rings, assembled 2+2+2, to the twist tie.

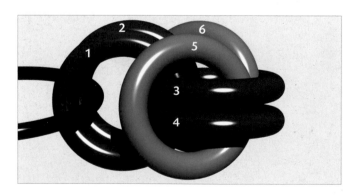

3. Fold back rings 5 and 6.

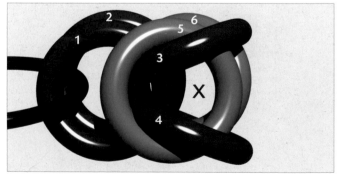

4. Open rings 3 and 4 to create a rectangular opening, marked above with an X.

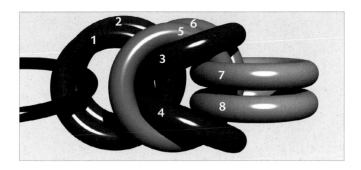

5. To assist in adding conector ring 7, press inward on the outside of rings 5 and 6 to hold the knot formation open. Add connector pair rings 7 and 8 through the rectangular opening in the knot formation.

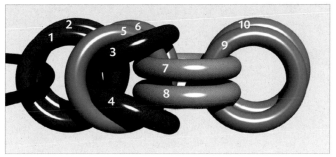

6. Add rings 9 and 10 to connector pair rings 7 and 8.

7. Add rings 11 and 12 to rings 9 and 10 to create a knot formation.

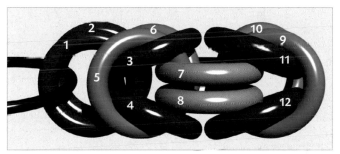

8. Fold back rings 11 and 12 and open rings 9 and 10 to create the rectangular opening. Press inward on the outside of rings 11 and 12 to hold the knot open.

9. Because the sequential knot formations mirror themselves, you must turn the chain upward by 90 degrees in order to see the rectangular opening, marked above with an X.

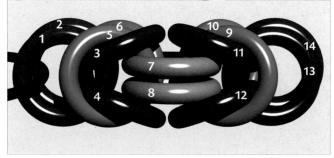

10. Add two jump rings through the rectangular opening in the knot formation, shown above as the blue 13 and 14 connector pair.

Assembly

I developed the following chain assembly technique by following the path of least resistance. This technique eliminates the need to put down the pliers and chain in order to pick up each new jump ring. At first it may seem to be a gymnastic feat, but with time and patience you will soon develop an efficient motion as the hand tools become extensions of your fingers. However, as you develop your chain-making skills, don't get lazy; speed is no substitute for consistency. Chain making is a repetitive process that combines right-brain creativity with left-brain number counting into a quiet, meditative, hands-on process.

Essential Hand Movements

The chain-making process requires dexterity and coordination. You must be able to hold and apply pressure to the pliers with your middle, ring, and pinky fingers, while using your thumb and index fingers as "pinchers." The pincher fingers pick up each jump ring, transfer it from hand to hand, and then transfer it to the pliers. The jump ring is then opened, added to the chain, and closed with a finishing file. Efficiency of motion will increase the speed of your chain making tenfold.

1. Pick up a jump ring with the right hand's thumb and index finger. Transfer the jump ring to the left hand's thumb and index finger. Note that the chain is being held in the left hand's pliers.

2. Transfer the jump ring from the left hand's thumb and index finger to the right hand's pliers, grasping the ring so that the (cut) opening is facing upward.

3. Grasp the chain with the right hand's thumb and index fingers while releasing the top ring from the chain with the left hand's pliers. Hold the jump ring between the two pliers and rotate your right hand away and your left hand toward you. Push, or pull, each pair of pliers with equal pressure and a gentle twisting action to create a gap wider than the rings it must pass through.

4. While holding the open jump ring in the left hand's pliers, add the ring to the chain by rotating your wrist in such a way as to hook the open end of the jump ring through the chain, like a fishhook.

5. Let the chain dangle from the open jump ring in the left hand's pliers, grab the jump ring again with the pliers in the right hand, and gently close the jump ring, flat and flush, with a twisting action.

6. Hold the closed ring in the left hand's pliers and use the flat file to smooth the top and inside of the jump ring's cut. If needed, use the round file to smooth the inside of the ring's cut by rotating the file in accordance with the action sequence.

Determining Length

Correctly determining the overall chain length affects not only the comfortable fit and wear but also the functionality of the jewelry piece. The goal is to balance the aesthetic preferences of the wearer while remaining within the determined maximum and minimum lengths.

Bracelets

When sizing a bracelet, there is a minimum and a maximum length. The minimum length is obtained by wrapping fabric measuring tape around the thinnest part of the wearer's wrist, directly behind the hand. Add an inch to this measurement to allow room to work the clasp and for comfort. The maximum length is determined by having the wearer hold his or her thumb under the hand and then wrapping fabric measuring tape around his or her knuckles. A bracelet's length must be slightly smaller than the maximum length so that it does not slide off the hand. Typically, a woman's bracelet is 7½ to 8 inches in length, while a man's ranges from 8½ to 10 inches in length.

When measuring a chain's length, always hold the chain by the clasp and let it hang while holding the fabric measuring tape. If you measure the chain flat on the tabletop, gravity will pull the chain down and thus slightly constrict its overall length.

Necklaces

When sizing a necklace, there is also an aesthetic minimum and maximum length. The minimum is obtained by wrapping fabric measuring tape around the base of the neck just above the collarbone and then adding an inch to allow room in order to work the clasp and wear it comfortably. Typically, a woman's necklace ranges from 14 to 16 inches in length for a choker, and up to 24 inches for a cascading necklace. A man's necklace is usually 17 to 19 inches in length.

Clasp Length   Chain Length   Catch Ring Length

Once you have determined the overall length for your bracelet or necklace, subtract the length of the clasp and catch rings to achieve the full length of chain for your project. The image above illustrates the division of an overall bracelet length into a clasp length, chain length, and catch ring length.

Evaluating Chains

After handcrafting a few inches of the Byzantine chain, evaluate your craftsmanship with the following two tests. The first test measures the linear spacing, or the gap, at the outside ring edge of the knot formation. The second test evaluates the chain's overall flexibility, or angle at which the chain bends at any given connector pair.

A correctly proportioned Byzantine chain's linear spacing will have just a slight gap between the outside ring edge of the knot formation, as seen in the chain pictured at right. This allows the knots to pass one another without touching or clicking. This chain's flexibility will bend at roughly 90 degrees at any given connector pair, as seen below right.

Test 1

If the knot formation's outside ring edges overlap, as seen in the chain pictured at right, or if the chain has limited flexibility and cannot bend at a right angle, as seen below right, your Byzantine chain is too tight to continue adding jump rings. There are four possible reasons: (1) the wire is too thick; (2) the mandrel diameter is too small; (3) the jump rings are cut short of a full circumference; or (4) some of the jump rings are not closed completely flat.

Test 2

On the other hand, your Byzantine chain will be too loose if there are large gaps in the linear spacing between the knot formations, as seen in the chain pictured at right, or if the chain is too flexible and the bend is greater than a right angle, as seen below right. There are four possible reasons: (1) the wire is too thin; (2) the diameter of the mandrel is too large; (3) the wire was wrapped with gaps that created oval rings; or (4) some of the rings are not closed completely flush.

Linear Designs

This chapter introduces four simple linear designs—the Zig-Zag Beading, Large Ring, Rosary, and Spade—of the Byzantine chain through five jewelry projects. We start with the classic Byzantine Chain, which can then be embellished with the Zig-Zag Beading design. The second design is the Large Ring, which allows large rings to be built into a Byzantine chain to support a variety of dangling, decorative charms. The third chain design is the Rosary, in which individual beads are encased and combined into the Byzantine chain. The chapter concludes with the fourth design, the Spade, and its variation, the Double Spade, which assembles brilliant gemstone beads within a Byzantine chain. In addition, this skill-building section includes a step by step introduction to bead reaming and looping techniques in the Rosary design project.

The Byzantine Chain

The Byzantine chain is the original linear chain pattern that serves as the basis for all of the designs presented in this book. Many of the projects begin with a pre-scribed length of Byzantine chain or call for segments of Byzantine chain. In the step-by-step instructions, the Byzantine chain will be referred to as the "chain". It is important that you take the time to master the fundamentals of the Byzantine construction before attempting more complex designs. Refer to pages 46–47 as needed.

To make an 8-inch bracelet, you will need one hundred-and-seventy 18-gauge Byzantine jump rings; three 14-gauge Byzantine catch rings; and one clasp.

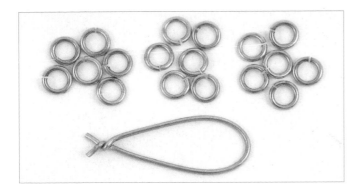

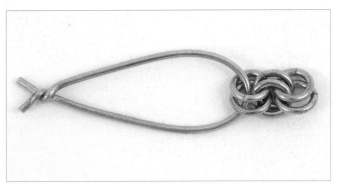

1. Arrange the 18-gauge jump rings into sets of six. (Make sure they are of good quality. *See* page 33.)

2. Make a twist tie out of a 3-inch scrap of wire. Add two rings to the twist tie. Add two more rings to the previous pair, 2+2. Add two more rings to the previous pair, 2+2+2.

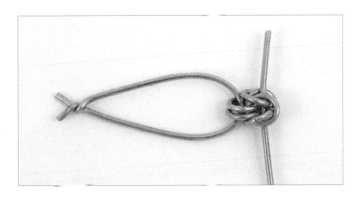

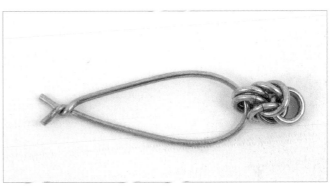

3. Fold back the top pair of rings and open the middle pair of rings to create a rectangular opening in the knot formation. Place a piece of scrap wire through the rectangular opening to hold the knot open.

4. Add two rings through the knot formation.

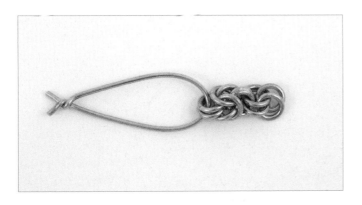

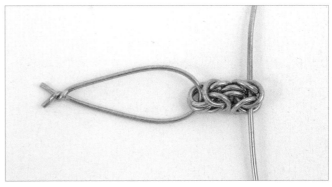

5. Add four more rings to the previous pair, 2+2+2.

6. Fold back the top pair of rings and open the middle pair of rings to create a rectangular opening in the knot formation. Place a piece of scrap wire through the rectangular opening to hold the knot open.

Zig-Zag Beading Design

The Zig-Zag design is simply a bead embellishment to the outside of the Byzantine chain. It is accomplished by attaching a length of beading wire to the end connector pair and securing it in place with a crimp bead. A wire is then weaved through the length of the chain as the beads are added. By using two sizes of beads, 3- and 6mm, the wire is able to flow through the chain without kinking and binding the chain's overall flexibility. The beads lie on opposite sides of the chain, creating a wide and flat finished chain.

To set an 8-inch Byzantine bracelet, you will need fourteen 6mm turquoise beads; twenty-eight 3mm hematite beads; two crimp beads; beading wire; two sets of chain-nose pliers; and side cutters.

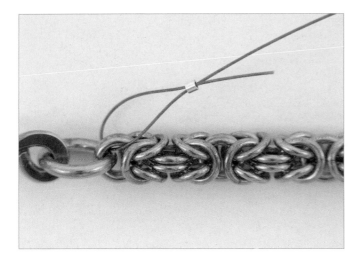

1. Cut a length of beading wire that is twice the length of the chain. Run one end of the beading wire through the end connector pair. Position the beading wire so that one end is an inch or two in length. Add a crimp bead to both ends of the wire.

2. Hold both ends of the beading wire with a pair of chain-nose pliers. Push the crimp head toward the connector pair with a second pair of chain-nose pliers. Smash the crimp bead as close to the chain as possible.

3. Thread one 3mm bead and one 6mm bead on both wires.

4. Cut off the shorter length of one beading wire—not both—just past the second bead with side cutters.

Note: The extra length of beading wire through the first two beads allows for the wire to stretch without pulling off the crimp bead.

5. Add the second 3mm bead. Push the end of the beading wire through the chain's third connector pair.

Pictured above is a detail of the beading wires passing through the Byzantine chain.

6. Add a 3mm bead, one 6mm bead, and a second 3mm bead to the beading wire. Run the wire's tip back through the chain's fifth connector pair.

7. Continue adding the three beads, alternating back and forth in a zig-zag sequence. Notice how the beading wire runs through every other connector pair when the chain lays flat on one side.

8. After adding the last bead sequence, add one crimp bead.

9. Run the end of the beading wire through the inside ring of the last knot formation, looping it around the end connector pair and back through the inside ring, the crimp bead, and the 3- and 6mm beads.

10. Pull the beading wire taut, taking care not to pull the wire too tightly, which will restrict the chain's overall flexibility. After the chain's flexibility has been checked (*see* page 51) and all the beads are snug against the chain, smash the crimp bead with chain-nose pliers to secure the beads. Snip off the excess beading wire just inside of the last set of 6mm beads. Be extra careful at this point to cut off only the excess wire and not the main wire holding the beads.

Large Ring Design

The Large Ring design places 14-gauge Byzantine jump rings between sections of an 18-gauge Byzantine chain to secure cascading charms. Strategically placed, these large rings break up the chain pattern and add an aesthetic openness. The number of rings and charms placed on the chain's length can be adjusted by changing the number of knot formations within the chain sections.

To make a 7½-inch bracelet, you will need one hundred-and-thirty 18-gauge Byzantine jump rings; seven 14-gauge Byzantine catch rings; and one clasp.

To maximize the number of charms to be fitted to the bracelet, add the 14-gauge rings to the connector pair of each knot formation. Notice that this odd number makes the large rings turn 90 degrees.

Adding the 14-gauge rings to the end connector pairs with two knot formations in between creates an aesthetically balanced chain. Notice that this even number makes the large rings lie flat.

Adding the 14-gauge rings to the end connector pairs with three knot formations in between creates a more spacious chain. Notice that this odd number of knot formations makes the large rings turn 90 degrees.

Adding the 14-gauge rings to the end connector pair with four knot formations in between, which was employed in the sample bracelet on the opposite page, creates a greater chain to large ring ratio that is counterbalanced with larger charms. Notice that this even number makes the large rings lie flat.

Charmed

The addition of 14-gauge large jump rings to an 18-gauge Byzantine chain facilitates the addition of charms. Charms are small figurines representing animals, hobbies, activities, keepsakes, and souvenirs. You can find a wide variety of cast metal charms through catalogue companies or at your local bead shop. The charms below were crafted out of metal clay by artist Sherri Haab. Alternatively, try adding old keys, an heirloom wedding ring, or seashells.

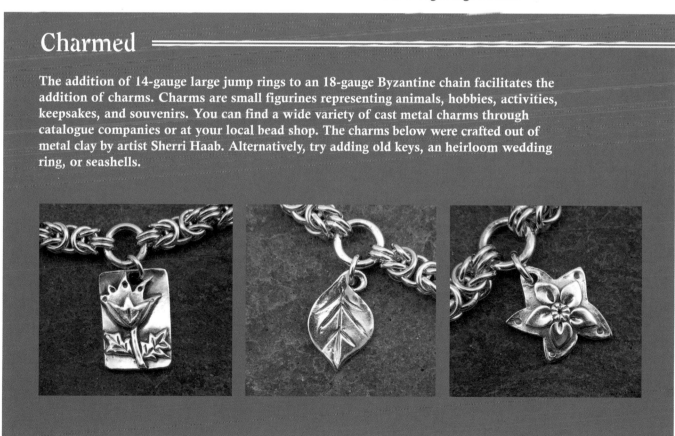

Rosary Design

The Rosary design allows the color and brilliance of gemstone beads to be assembled into a length of Byzantine chain. For each Rosary bead setting, a length of 18-gauge wire is passed through a bead. The two wire ends are then formed into double loops to encase the bead. Four jump rings are added to each double loop, assembled 2+2, creating two knot formations that can be joined by connector pairs. The chain between each Rosary setting can be lengthened as desired to make a more spacious sequence of beads throughout the length of chain. We will first learn about bead reaming and consistent looping before we make the Rosary design.

To make a 16-inch necklace, you will need two hundred and thirty-eight 18-gauge Byzantine jump rings; three 14-gauge Byzantine catch rings; and one clasp. The bead setting requires eight 3-inch lengths of 18-gauge wire; eight 6mm carnelian beads; round-nose pliers; and side cutters.

Bead Reaming

The Rosary design and Spade design (*see* page 68) both require that a 1.02mm 18-gauge wire pass through the drilled hole within the bead. This can be problematic if (1) the wire thickness is too big or the drilled hole is too small—in which case the wire can be physically pulled down with a drawplate to a smaller diameter or the hole can be enlarged with a bead reamer—and (2) if there is a flaw inside the bead and the drilled holes do not align. Gemstone beads are typically drilled from both ends. Sometimes the hole is bent if the two drill holes are not aligned. If this is the case, their unaligned angles can be removed with a bead reamer. Depending on the hardness of the gemstone, the process can range from easy to impossible.

A bead reamer is a tapered metal bit that is plated with fine diamond chips. The bit is attached to an electric screwdriver's three-prong chuck. To reduce the heat and friction that causes the bead to break, keep the bead and bit wet and cool by placing them under dripping water. Apply the bit to the bead in successive attempts, easing off to allow the water to wash away the removed mineral material off the bit while flushing out the bead's hollow tube.

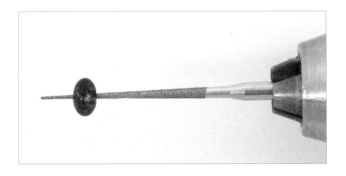

Use a bead reamer to enlarge the diarmeter of the bead's hole.

Consistent Looping

The Rosary and Spade designs both allow pre-drilled gemstone beads to be set into a Byzantine chain by passing a length of wire through the bead and encasing it within double loops. These loops serve as the bottom pair to build the chain sections between each rosary or spade. For the double loop to correspond with the 18-gauge Byzantine jump rings, it has to be the same diameter. To obtain the true diameter, close one jump ring flat and flush. Place the jump ring on the jaw of round-nose pliers. With the jump ring in place, use the edge of the flat file to groove a shallow notch into the jaws of the round-nose pliers on both sides of the jump ring. The true diameter is the space between the notches. When you wrap the double loops, simply keep adding the wire between the two notches, which will make your double loops the same diameter as the Byzantine chain built from them.

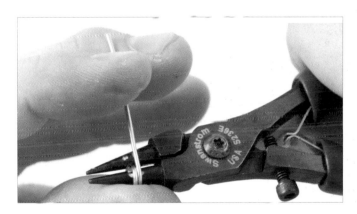

1. To obtain the true diameter of the double loops, close one jump ring flat and flush. Place the jump ring on the jaw of round-nose pliers.

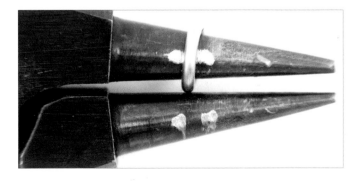

2. Groove a shallow notch into the jaws of the round-nose pliers on both sides of the jump ring.

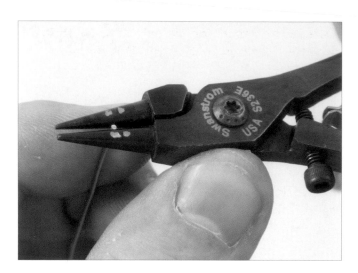

3. Cut the wire into 3-inch sections. Hold one end of the wire in the round-nose pliers and position it between the filed notches in the jaws.

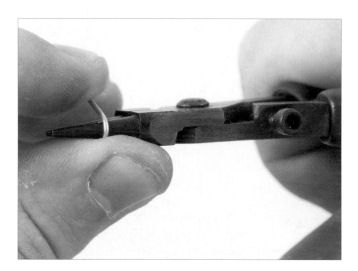

4. Bend the wire around the jaw toward you, applying pressure to where the wire is bending. As the first loop is forming, guide the wire on an angle to the starting point so that the wire will not overlap.

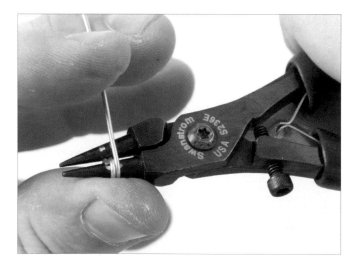

5. Release pressure from the pliers, allowing the loop to rotate down. Regrip the loop and continue wrapping the wire twice around the jaw between the filed notches.

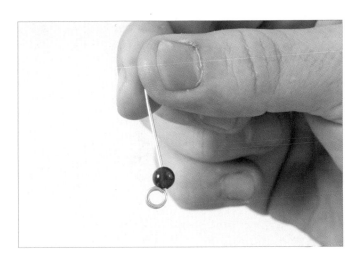

6. Add the bead to the wire. If the bead won't fit on the wire, *see* Bead Reaming on page 63.

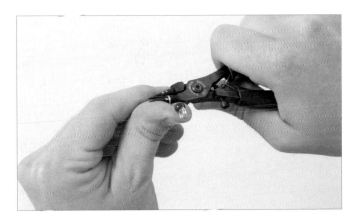

7. Wrap the second double loop with the round-nose pliers, keeping the wire wrapped between the filed notches.

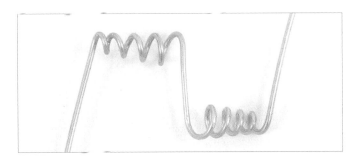

To obtain a symmetrical bead setting, the double loops must be wrapped in an opposite rotation and direction.

8. Complete two full loops, which requires a third reposition. Wrap all the wire in order to snugly encase the bead between the two loops.

9. Trim off the excess wire at a 45-degree angle with side cutters, being careful not to cut the double loop.

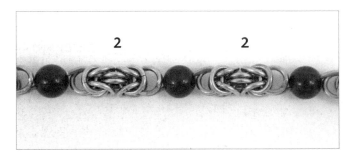

10. Add four jump rings to each double loop, assembled 2+2, creating two open knot sequences—one on each side. Fold into knot formations.

At this point, attaching each knot formation to a connector pair creates a sequence with two knot formations between each rosary bead.

11. Add six jump rings to each side, assembled 2+2+2, creating two open knot sequences on each side of the rosary bead. Fold into knot formations.

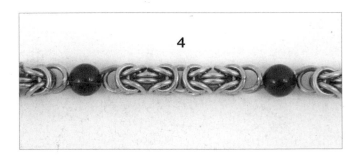

At this point, attaching each knot formation to a connector pair creates a sequence with four knot formations between each rosary bead.

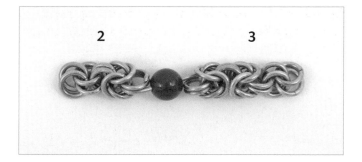

12. Add six jump rings to one side so that one side has three open knot sequences and the other side has two open knot sequences. Fold into knot formations.

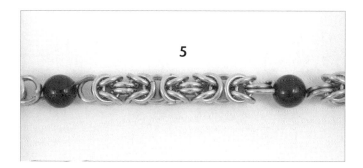

Attaching these chain sections to the connector pair creates a sequence with five knot formations between each rosary bead.

Rosary Bead Set

For my elder brother's christening into the Catholic Church, I handcrafted a 26-inch rosary, set with 6mm and 8mm hematite gemstones and a cast pendant of the crucifix. While researching the project, I discovered that there is a specific sequence to the bead placement throughout the length of rosary chain. This sequence is accommodated by varying lengths of double chain between each rosary bead, creating a three-decade rosary.

Each decade is a sequence of ten 6mm beads, with two connector jump rings between each wrapped bead. Between each decade, a larger 8mm bead is spaced from the decades by six connector jump rings on both sides, assembled 2+2+2 in the double chain sequence. The rosary length is combined with a three-way cast pendant of the Blessed Virgin Mary, which allows a third length of chain to hang down. This second chain section contains five beads, ending with a crucifix in the following sequence:

3-way, 6 rings, 8mm, 6 rings, 6mm, 2 rings, 6mm, 2 rings, 6mm, 6 rings, 8mm, 8 rings, crucifix.

Spade Design

The Spade design enables beads to be assembled onto a length of Byzantine chain. To make this bead setting, a length of wire is passed through a bead. One wire end is flattened to prevent the bead from sliding off, while the other end is wrapped into a double loop to encase the bead. The double loop allows the two open knot sequences to be added to each side. The open knot sequences are then angled open and attached to a connector pair to create a length of chain. The chain segments between each setting can be lengthened if desired.

To make an 8-inch bracelet, you will need round-nose pliers; side cutters; needle file; sanding pad; one hundred and forty-two 18-gauge Byzantine jump rings; three 14-gauge Byzantine jump rings; and one clasp. The bead setting requires fourteen 18-gauge Byzantine jump ring spacers; fourteen 1 5/8-inch lengths of beading wire; and twenty-eight 6mm discus-shaped lapis lazuli beads.

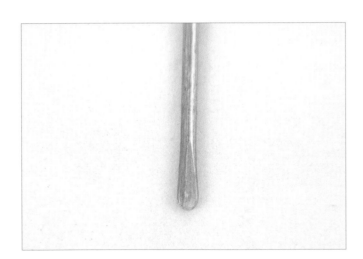

1. Cut the wire into 1 5/8-inch sections. Flatten the tip of the wire with a hammer and anvil.

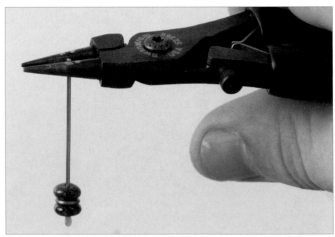

2. Smooth and round the tip with a needle file and sanding pad. Add one 6mm lapis lazuli bead, one jump ring spacer, and one lapis lazuli bead.

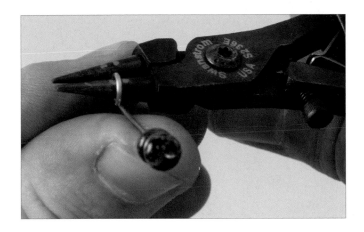

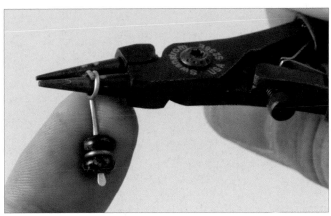

3. Hold the end of the wire section in the round-nose pliers and position the wire between the filed notches of the jaws (*see* page 63). Bend the wire around the jaw, applying pressure where the wire bends. As the first loop is forming, guide the wire at an angle near to the starting point.

4. Release pressure from the pliers, allowing the loop to rotate down. Regrip the loop and continue wrapping the wire twice around the jaw between the filed notches.

5. Finish with a double loop held snugly against the bead.

6. Snip off any excess wire with side cutters at a 45-degree angle.

7. Add eight jump rings to the double loop, assembled 2+2, on each side to create two open knot sequences.

8. Fold back and open knot sequence. Attach each spade formation to a connector pair to create a length of chain.

Double Spade Variation

The Double Spade variation allows twice the number of beads to be set onto a Byzantine chain. To accomplish this, a length of wire is passed through two sets of beads, which are then flattened on both sides to keep from falling off. The middle of the wire is wrapped into a double loop that encases the beads on both sides. This double loop serves as a base pair to add two open knot sequences that can be joined to a connector pair and added to the Byzantine chain.

You will need round-nose pliers; side cutters; hammer and anvil; file; sanding pad; fifty-six discus-shaped beads; twenty-eight jump ring spacers; and a length of 18-gauge wire.

1. Cut the wire into 1 ⅝-inch length sections. Flatten the tip of the wire with a hammer and anvil. Smooth and round the tip with a file and sanding pad. Add two beads and a jump ring spacer.

2. Add a second set of beads and a jump ring spacer.

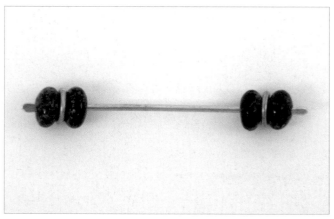

3. Flatten and round the second wire tip. Separate the pairs of beads.

4. While holding the middle of the wire in the round-nose pliers, bend the wire until both sets of beads are parallel.

5. Continue to bend the middle of the wire, allowing the bead sets to overlap.

6. Wrap both ends until the bead sets come around and touch.

7. Add eight jump rings, assembled 2+2, to both sides of the double spade formation, creating two open knots.

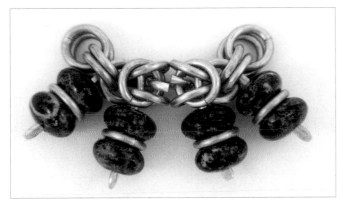

8. Attach two double spade formations to a connector pair.

9. Attach a third double spade formation and combine the design into a finished Byzantine chain.

Twisted Spade

To put a spin on the Spade design, try twisting the double spade formation instead of wrapping it. This allows the beads to hang lower and turn slightly up, giving an organic feel, like that of grapes on a vine.

1. Start at step 5 on page 70.

2. While holding the middle loop with the round-nose pliers, twist the bead sets around, being careful not to break the beads.

3. Attach two open knot sequences to each twisted spade formation. Attach the open knot sequences to connector pairs in the Byzantine chain.

Additive
Designs

This chapter introduces four unique designs and two variations: the Large Knot, Side Knot, Crown, Crown Bead Variation, Bi-Crown, and Bi-Crown Bead Variation, through six jewelry projects. The Large Knot chain pattern utilizes a series of large rings to replace a knot formation in the Byzantine chain design, enhancing the visual rhythm and texture. The Side Knot is essentially a large knot that has been rotated 45 degrees to connect to the Byzantine chain at alternate points, creating an elongated knot formation. The Crown and Bi-Crown designs add sequentially placed, perpendicular crown formations to the Byzantine chain, resulting in chains with great depth and beauty.

Large Knot Design

The Large Knot design is a Byzantine chain pattern with sequentially placed large knot formations, each constructed out of four 14-gauge Byzantine jump rings. These 14-gauge knot formations lie between two sections of 18-gauge Byzantine chain, which break up the continuous chain into sections and add aesthetic weight to the chain pattern.

To make a 15-inch necklace, you will need three hundred and twenty 18-gauge Byzantine jump rings; thirty-nine 14-gauge Byzantine catch rings; and one clasp.

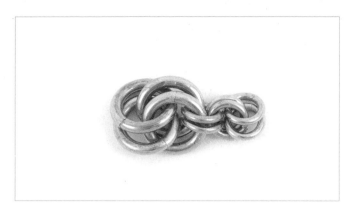

1. Join four 14-gauge rings, assembled 2+2. Add six 18-gauge rings, assembled 2+2+2, to two of the 14-gauge rings.

2. Fold back the large knot formation and hold it open with a piece of scrap wire.

3. Add six 18-gauge rings, assembled 2+2+2, to the opposite side of the large knot formation to create open knot sequences on both sides of the large knot.

Attaching the individual large knot formations to an 18-gauge Byzantine connector pair creates two 18-gauge knots between each large knot formation. Notice that the large knots face in opposite directions.

Small segments of the Large Knot design pattern can be attached to earring backs to make a set of earrings to match your necklace.

4. Add six 18-gauge rings, assembled 2+2+2, to one side of the large knot formation to create two 18-gauge knots on one side and one knot on the other side of the formation.

Combining these individual large knot formations with an 18-gauge Byzantine connector pair creates three 18-gauge knots between each large knot formation. Notice that the large knots face in the same direction.

5. Add six 18-gauge rings, assembled 2+2+2, to one side of the large knot formation to create two 18-gauge knots on one side and two knots on the other side of the formation.

Combining these individual large knot formations with an 18-gauge Byzantine connector pair creates four 18-gauge knots between each large knot formation. Notice that the large knots face in opposite directions.

6. Add six 18-gauge rings, assembled 2+2+2, to one side of the large knot formation to create two 18-gauge knots on one side and three knots on the other side of the formation.

Combining these individual large knot formations with an 18-gauge Byzantine connector pair creates five 18-gauge knots between each large knot formation. Notice that the large knots face in the same direction.

Side Knot Design

The Side Knot design is a linear chain pattern with sequentially placed large knot formations that are constructed from four 14-gauge Byzantine rings that sit between sections of 18-gauge Byzantine chain. The Side Knot design is similar to the Large Knot design (*see* pages 74–76), except that it is rotated 45 degrees and is attached to the side of the chain. There are four points on the side knot formation where you can attach the Byzantine chain. Be consistent as to which two polar points you add the Byzantine jump rings to. The length of the chain sections between the side knot formations can be adjusted as desired to create a more spacious or weighted design.

To make an 8-inch bracelet, you will need one hundred and fifty-eight 18-gauge Byzantine jump rings; twenty-three 14-gauge Byzantine catch rings; one clasp; and two pieces of scrap wire.

1. Add four 14-gauge rings, assembled 2+2, to a twist-tie.

2. Fold back the knot formation and hold it open with a piece of scrap wire.

3. Add three 18-gauge rings through the rectangular opening in the 14-gauge knot formation.

4. Add three 18-gauge rings through the rectangular opening in the 14-gauge knot formation that are parallel to the twist-tie. Remove the twist-tie.

5. Add two 18-gauge rings to the 14-gauge side knot formation where the rings overlap.

6. Add four 18-gauge rings, assembled 2+2, to the previously added pair to create an open knot sequence on both sides of the side knot formation.

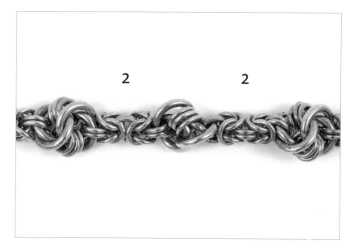

7. Attach the individual side knot formations to an 18-gauge Byzantine connector pair to create two 18-gauge knots between each side knot formation.

8. Add six 18-gauge rings, assembled 2+2+2, to one side of the Side Knot formation to create two 18-gauge knots on one side of the formation and one knot on the other side. Combining these Side Knot chain sections creates a linear chain with three 18-gauge knots between each side knot formation.

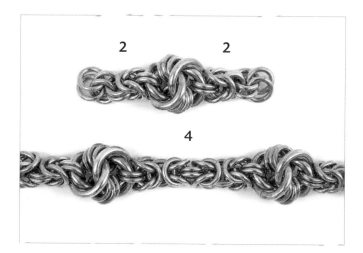

9. Add six 18-gauge rings, assembled 2+2+2, to the opposite side of the side knot formation to create two 18-gauge knots on both sides of the formation. Combining these Side Knot chain sections creates a linear chain with four 18-gauge knots between each side knot formation.

10. Add six 18-gauge jump rings, assembled 2+2+2, to the side knot formation to create two 18-gauge knots on one side of the formation and three knots on the other side. Combining these side knot formations creates a linear chain with five 18-gauge knots between each side knot formation.

Crown Design

The Crown design is a Byzantine chain pattern enhanced with sequentially placed crown formations. To make a crown formation, you simply add four jump rings, assembled 2+2, to every other connector pair in a Byzantine chain, creating open knot sequences. These open knot sequences are then folded back and finished with two 18-gauge jump rings. The crown formations are added to only one side of the Byzantine chain, so that they face in the same direction and do not twist the chain. Crown formations add visual weight as well as a repetitive texture to the finished chain.

To make an 8-inch bracelet, you will need two hundred and fifty-two 18-gauge Byzantine jump rings; three 14-gauge Byzantine catch rings; and one clasp.

1. Start with a length of 18-gauge Byzantine chain. Add four 18-gauge rings, assembled 2+2, to every other connector pair in the Byzantine chain. Make sure all of the open knot sequences face in the same direction and do not twist the chain.

Pictured above is a close-up of the open knot sequence.

2. Fold back each open knot sequence. Tuck the outside rings into their neighboring knots in the Byzantine chain. This creates a wide rectangular opening, which allows room to add a pair of finishing rings.

3. Add a pair of finishing rings through the open knot sequence's rectangular opening to complete the crown formation. The crown formation's outside rings can now be untucked to sit on the outside of their neighboring knots in the Byzantine chain.

The completed Crown design.

Crown Bead Variation

The Crown Bead Variation allows the two finishing jump rings of the crown formation (*see* pages 80–81) to secure beading wire and beads. The beading wire runs parallel to the Byzantine chain, traveling through the two finishing jump rings of each crown formation, with an 8mm bead saddled between each formation. The end of each beading wire is passed through a plug bead and a crimp bead to secure the wire in place. Because the crown formations are added to only one side of the Byzantine chain, the beads create a wide bracelet that lies flat on the wrist, with the beads protruding outward. As you set the final plug bead, do not pull the beading wire too tightly, or it will restrict the flexibility of the chain.

To set an 8-inch bracelet, you will need thirteen 8mm amethyst beads; two 3mm amethyst beads; two crimp beads; beading wire; and two sets of chain-nose pliers.

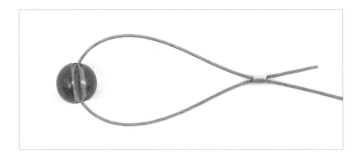

1. Cut a length of beading wire that is 1 ¹/₂ times longer than the length of the Byzantine chain. (In this project we will use 12 inches for an 8-inch bracelet.) Add one crimp bead and one 3mm plug bead to the beading wire. Run the end of the beading wire back through the crimp bead, creating a loop with the plug bead in the middle of the loop.

2. Hold both ends of the beading wire in one set of chain-nose pliers and push the crimp bead toward the plug bead with a second set of chain-nose pliers. Smash the crimp bead as close to the plug bead as possible. Leave at least 1 inch of beading wire on the short end.

3. Place both ends of the beading wire through the two finishing rings of the first crown formation. Add one 8mm bead to each end of the beading wire.

4. Cut off the shorter length of beading wire just past the first 8mm bead—not both wires, just one.

Note: Leaving an extra length of beading wire through the first bead allows the wire to stretch without the crimp bead falling off.

5. Run the beading wire through the finishing rings of the second crown formation. Add a second 8mm bead. Continue running the beading wire through the finishing rings of each crown formation, followed by a bead, along the length of the chain.

6. After passing through the last crown formation, add a crimp bead and a 3mm plug bead to both beading wire leads. Loop the beading wires back through the crimp bead and through the last 8mm bead. Pull the beading wire tightly, but be careful not to restrict the flexibility of the chain.

7. After the chain's flexibility has been checked (*see* page 51) and both plug beads are snug against the outside crown formations, smash the crimp bead with the chain-nose pliers to secure the beads.

8. Snip off the excess beading wire just inside the last 8mm bead. Be extra careful at this point to cut only the excess wire and not the main wire holding the beads.

Bi-Crown Design

Much like the Crown design (*see* pages 80–81), the Bi-Crown design enhances a Byzantine chain with sequentially placed crown formations. However, the Bi-Crown design differs from the Crown in that the crown formations run along two sides of the chain instead of just one side. To achieve this, open knot sequences are added to every connector pair on two adjoining sides of the four-sided Byzantine chain. Bi-crown formations add a visual weight, pattern, and texture to the finished chain.

To make an 8-inch bracelet, you will need three hundred and thirty-two 18-gauge Byzantine jump rings; three 14-gauge Byzantine catch rings; and one clasp.

1. Start with a length of 18-gauge Byzantine chain. Add four 18-gauge rings, assembled 2+2, to every connector pair in the Byzantine chain so that all of the open knot sequences are built onto two sides of the chain.

2. Fold back each open knot sequence. Tuck the outside rings into their neighboring knots on the Byzantine chain. This creates a wide rectangular opening, which allows room to add two finishing rings.

3. Add two finishing rings through the open knot sequence's rectangular opening to complete the crown formation. The crown formations's outside rings can now be untucked to sit on the outside of their neighboring knots on the Byzantine chain.

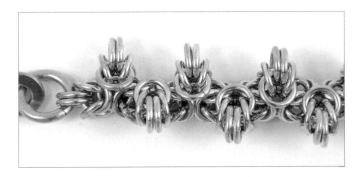

The completed Bi-Crown design.

Bi-Crown Bead Variation

The Bi-Crown Bead Variation allows the two finishing jump rings of each crown formation (*see page 81*) to secure beading wire and beads. The beading wire runs runs parallel to the Byzantine chain, traveling through the two finishing jump rings of each crown formation, with an 8mm bead saddled between each formation. The end of each beading wire is passed through a plug bead and a crimp bead to secure the wire in place. Because the crown formations are added to two sides of the four-sided Byzantine chain, the gemstones create a wide bracelet that lies flat on the wrist, with the beads protruding outward. As you set the final plug bead, do not pull the beading wire too tightly, or it will restrict the flexibility of the chain.

To set an 8-inch bracelet, you will need twenty-five 8mm clear glass beads; four 3mm clear glass beads; four crimp beads; beading wire, and two sets of chain-nose pliers.

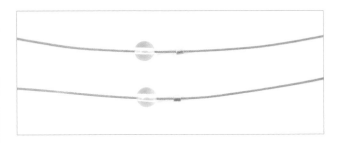

1. Cut two lengths of beading wire 1 ½ times longer than the length of chain. (In this project we will use 12 inches for an 8-inch bracelet.) Add one crimp bead and one 3mm plug bead to each wire.

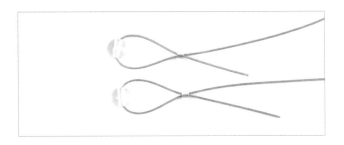

2. Run the end of the beading wire back through the crimp bead, creating a loop with the plug bead in the middle of the loop.

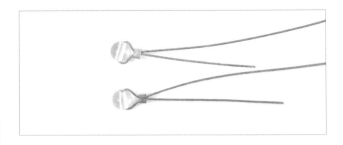

3. With chain-nose pliers, smash the crimp bead as close to the plug bead as possible, making sure to leave at least 1 inch of beading wire on the short end.

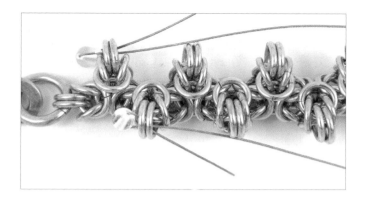

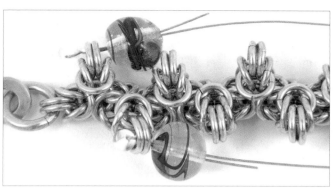

4. Place both ends of the beading wire through the two finishing rings of the first two crown formations.

5. Add one 8mm bead to both ends of the beading wire.

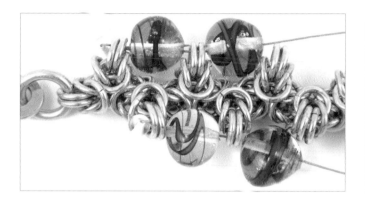

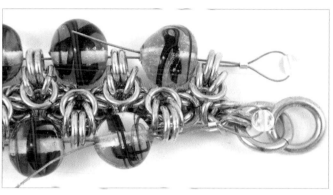

6. Cut off the shorter lengths of the beading wires just past the first beads—not both wires, just one. Run the beading wire through the finishing rings of the next crown formations. Add a second pair of 8mm beads.

7. Continue running the beading wires through each crown formation, followed by a bead. After passing through the last crown formation, add a crimp bead and a 3mm plug bead to both beading wire leads. Loop the wires back through the crimp bead and then through the last 8mm bead.

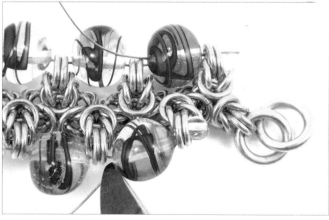

8. Pull the beading wire tightly until all four plug beads are snug against the outside crown formations. Smash the crimp bead with chain-nose pliers to secure the beads.

9. Snip off the excess beading wire just inside the last 8mm bead. Be extra careful at this point to cut only the excess wire and not the main wire holding the beads.

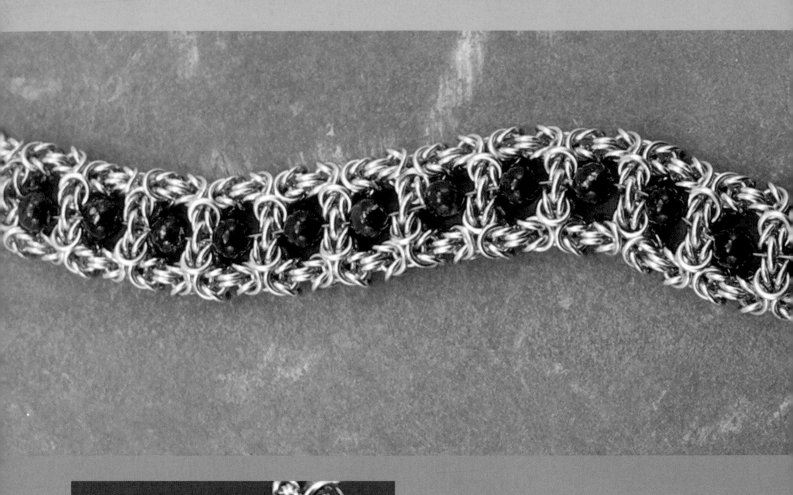

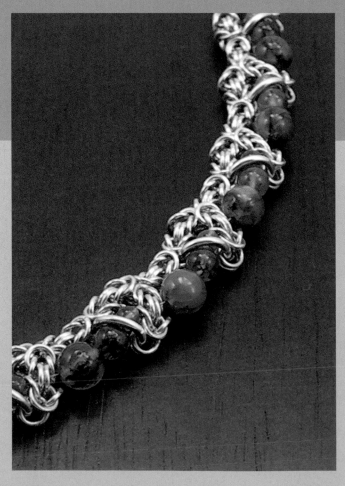

Combined
Designs

In this chapter we will build upon the previously discussed chain-making techniques and make exciting dimensional jewelry. We begin with the Parallel Bead design, which is a beading technique that incorporates a strand of beads into the Byzantine chain. The second design is the Wave, which allows an extension to be arched into the Byzantine chain with a large catch ring, creating a hollow, conical wave formation that can then be embellished with the Wave Bead Variation. The next design is the Half-Square, in which the Crown design is suspended by a sequence of large catch rings. The Half-Square can also be enhanced with the Half-Square Bead Variation. Finally, the chapter concludes with the Square design, in which two lengths of Byzantine chains are connected, creating hollow, square spaces. The Square Bead Variation balances the chain with a beaded embellishment.

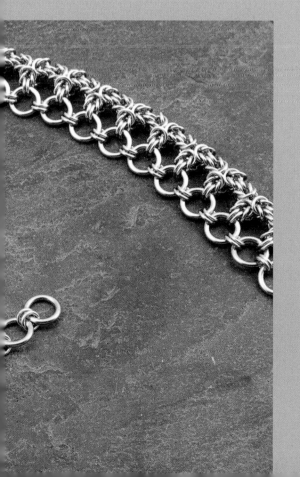

Parallel Bead Design

1. Start with a length of 18-gauge Byzantine chain. Add one 18-gauge jump ring to every other connector pair in the Byzantine chain so that all of the rings face in the same direction and do not twist the chain.

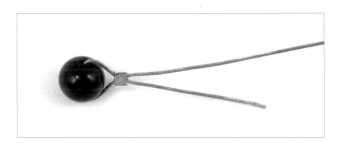

2. Cut a length of beading wire that is 1 ½ times longer than the length of the chain. Add one crimp bead and one 4 mm plug bead to the wire. Run the end of the beading wire back through the crimp bead, creating a loop with the plug bead in the middle of the loop. Hold both ends of the beading wire in one set of chain-nose pliers and push the crimp bead toward the plug bead with the second set of chain-nose pliers. Smash the crimp bead as close to the plug bead as possible. Leave at least 1 inch of beading wire on the short end.

The Parallel Set design is a Byzantine chain enhanced with sequentially placed loops that support a strand of 6mm beads. Single 18-gauge jump rings are added to every other connector pair to create perpendicular loops that hold the beading wire, which in turn supports the beads. Note that all of the loops are added to only one side of the chain and face in the same direction. This allows the strand of beads to lie flat without twisting the chain.

To make an 8-inch bracelet, you will need one hundred and ninety-seven 18-gauge Byzantine jump rings; three 14-gauge Byzantine catch rings; and one clasp. The bead setting requires twenty-six 6mm black onyx beads; two 4mm black onyx beads; two crimp beads; thirteen ring spacers; two sets of chain-nose pliers; and beading wire.

3. Run both ends of the beading wire through the first ring.

4. Add a 6 mm bead, a ring spacer, and a second 6mm bead. Snip off the excess wire just past the second 6mm bead.

5. Run the beading wire through the next ring. Add a 6mm bead, a ring spacer, and a second 6mm bead. Continue running the beading wire through each ring, adding a set of beads and a ring spacer along the chain's length.

6. After passing through the last ring, add a crimp bead and a 4mm plug bead to the beading wire. Loop the beading wires back through the crimp bead, passing it through the last set of 6mm beads.

7. Pull the beading wire tightly, without restricting its flexibility, so that the Byzantine chain curves into a gentle arc. After the flexibility has been checked (*see* page 51) and both plug beads are snug against the outside loops, smash the crimp bead with the chain-nose pliers to secure the beads.

8. Snip off the excess beading wire just inside the last set of 6mm beads. Be extra careful at this point to cut off only the excess wire and not the main wire holding the beads.

Wave Design

Similar to the rhythmic rise and fall of ocean waves, the Wave design features sequentially placed wave formations that rise and fall on a Byzantine chain. The waves are essentially crown formations (*see* pages 80–81) that have been doubled in length and attached to every fourth connector pair with a 14-gauge Inca puño jump ring. The wave formations are added to only one side of the four-sided chain so that they face in the same direction without twisting the chain. The wave formations create spaces that can be left empty or filled with beads to enhance the design (*see* pages 94–95).

To make an 8 ½-inch bracelet, you will need two hundred and seventy-two 18-gauge Byzantine jump rings; seven 14-gauge Inca puño catch rings; three 14-gauge Byzantine catch rings; and one clasp.

1. Attach four 18-gauge rings, assembled 2+2, to every fourth connector pair in the Byzantine chain. Make sure that the open knot sequences face in the same direction and do not twist the chain.

2. Fold back each open knot sequence and attach two finishing rings to complete the crown formation.

3. Attach four 18-gauge rings, assembled 2+2. Fold them back and add two more rings to complete the extension.

4. Attach one 14-gauge Inca puño ring through the extension's finishing pair of rings and the skipped connector pair on the Byzantine chain, which will allow the wave formations to face in the same direction and not twist the chain.

Notice that the crown formation's outside rings must sit on the outside of their neighboring knots in the Byzantine chain. This enables the chain extension to bend at a smooth angle, as it is suspended from—and attached—to the chain with a 14-gauge Inca puño jump ring.

Wave Bead Variation

Each wave formation in the Wave chain design (*see* pages 92–93) creates a hollow, cone-shaped space that looks stunning when set with beads. The beading wire runs parallel to the Byzantine chain. A sequence of 4-, 6-, and 8mm beads is embedded within each wave formation. The repetitive pattern of the bead sequence complements the fluid motion and rhythm of the chain. Due to the quantity of beads used to create this design, I prefer to use translucent gemstones, such as the moss agate seen in the example to the left. I feel opaque beads would add too much visual weight.

To set an 8 ½-inch bracelet, you will need eight 8mm, eight 6mm, and eight 4mm moss agate beads; two crimp beads; beading wire; and two sets of chain-nose pliers.

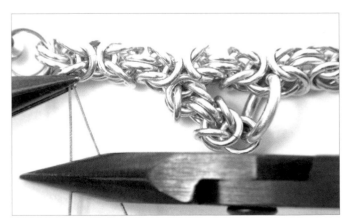

1. Cut a length of beading wire that is 1 ½ times longer than the length of chain and add a crimp bead. Loop the wire around the end connector pair and back through the crimp bead. Run both wires through the inside of the ring in the first knot formation.

2. Hold both ends of the beading wire in one set of chain-nose pliers and push the crimp bead toward the connector pair with the second set of pliers. Smash the crimp bead as close to the end connector pair as possible. Leave at least 1 inch of beading wire on the short end.

3. Add a sequence of one 4-, 6-, and 8mm beads to both ends of the beading wire. Cut off the excess wire, just past the 8mm bead. Be sure to cut just one wire—not both.

4. Run the beading wire through the center connector pair in the chain extension of the wave formation.

5. Add a second sequence of one 4-, 6-, and 8mm bead each to the beading wire. Continue running the beading wire alternately through each wave formation as you add another sequence of beads down the Byzantine chain.

6. After adding the last sequence of beads, add a crimp bead. Run the beading wire through the end connector pair, back through the crimp bead, and then though the last 8mm bead. Pull the beading wire taut, but be careful not to pull the wire too tightly, which will restrict the chain's overall flexibility.

7. After the chain's flexibility has been checked (*see* page 51) and all the beads are snug in their waves, smash the crimp bead with the chain-nose pliers to secure the beads. Snip off the excess beading wire just inside the last set of 6mm beads. Be extra careful at this point to cut off only the excess wire and not the main wire holding the beads.

Half-Square Design

The Half-Square design is a variation of the Crown design (*see* pages 80–81). However, the Byzantine chain is suspended from each crown formation's finishing pair of jump rings with a 14-gauge Inca puño catch ring. The 14-gauge Inca puño catch ring is then attached to two 18-gauge jump rings, creating a length of large rings that run parallel to the Byzantine chain. The last knots on both ends of the Byzantine chain are turned 90 degrees upward and serve as end crown formations. Therefore, we start attaching the crown formations at the fourth connector pair from both ends of the Byzantine chain. The simplicity of the large rings creates an attractive counterpoint to the complex Byzantine knot formations.

To make a 16-inch necklace, you will need six hundred and sixteen 18-gauge Byzantine jump rings; thirty-nine 14-gauge Inca puño catch rings; and one clasp.

1. Build crown formations onto every other connector pair in the Byzantine chain. Skip the second connector pair, as the first knot formation will be turned 90 degrees upward and serve as the first crown formation, as well as the end of the chain.

2. Attach an S-clasp to a 14-gauge Inca puño catch ring. Then attach a second 14-gauge Inca puño catch ring to the previous ring and the end connector pair in the Byzantine chain. Finally, attach two 18-gauge rings.

3. Attach a 14-gauge Inca puño catch ring to the pair of 18-gauge Byzantine jump rings you added in step 2 and to the next crown formation's finishing pair of rings. Then add two 18-gauge jump rings.

4. Attach another 14-gauge Inca puño catch ring and repeat step 3.

5. Continue this sequence of connecting a 14-gauge Inca puño catch ring to three pairs of 18-gauge rings.

6. When you reach the end of the chain, turn the last knot formation upward to create the final crown formation. Connect it to the 14-gauge Inca puño catch ring. Finish with a double catch ring, or extend the length for a smooth necklace backing.

Half-Square Bead Variation

The Half-Square design (*see* pages 96–97) creates a sequence of triangular-shaped spaces between the crown formations and Inca puño catch rings. The Half-Square Bead Variation fills these spaces with beads—in this project we will use freshwater pearls. The sample necklace has been set with freshwater potato pearls. The term potato refers to the oblong shape of these pearls, which are considered to have an undesirable quality in grading commercial pearls. However, the potato shape works perfectly with the Half-Square design, completing each triangular-shaped space. Although these pearls would be labeled 5mm in size, their height ranges from 5.5 to 6mm, making each pearl unique. The beading wire runs parallel to the chain and through the crown formation's final pair of jump rings, cradling a bead between each crown formation. A crimp bead is then smashed on each end of the beading wire to secure the beads in place. The simple, organic, and asymmetrical nature of the potato pearls complements the intricacy of the chain design, offering a simple, yet complex balance that I always find appealing.

To set a 16-inch necklace, you will need thirty 4mm freshwater pearls; two crimp beads; beading wire; and two sets of chain-nose pliers.

1. Start with a finished Half-Square chain design. Cut a length of beading wire that is 1 1/2 times longer than the length of chain and add a crimp bead. Loop the wire around the end connector pair and back through the crimp bead. Hold both of the beading wire ends in one set of chain-nose pliers and push the crimp bead toward the connector pair. Smash the crimp bead as close to the connector pair as possible.

2. Add one bead. Run the beading wire through the next crown formation's finishing pair of rings. Continue running the wire through each crown formation's finishing pair of rings, adding beads.

3. After adding the last bead, add a crimp bead.

4. Loop the beading wire through the last crown formation's finishing pair of rings and back through the crimp bead. Pull the wire taut, but not so tightly as to restrict the chain's overall flexibility. After the chain's flexibility has been checked (*see* page 51) and all the beads are in place, smash the crimp bead with the chain-nose pliers to secure the beads. Snip off the excess beading wire just inside the last beads, or inside the smashed crimp bead. Be extra careful at this point to cut off only the excess wire and not the main wire holding the beads.

Square Design

The Square design is essentially two Byzantine chains that are joined by attaching two opposite crown formations. Each chain is built as a Crown design (*see* pages 80–81) with the crown formations left in the open knot sequences. A 16-gauge Double jump ring runs through both crown formations and then attaches the two chains, creating a sequence of square spaces that can be filled with round beads (*see* pages 102–103) or left open. The finished Square design is quite wide, so it is tapered at both ends before the clasp is added.

To make a 7 ½-inch bracelet, you will need three hundred and seventy-eight 18-gauge Byzantine jump rings; seven 14-gauge Byzantine catch rings; twelve 16-gauge Double jump rings; and one clasp.

1. Start with two lengths of 18-gauge Byzantine chain. Add four 18-gauge rings, assembled 2+2, to every other connector pair in the Byzantine chain so that all of the open knot sequences face in the same direction and do not twist the chain.

2. Fold back both adjacent open knot sequences and tuck the crown formation's outside rings inside the Byzantine chain's neighboring knots in order to make a wider rectangular opening. Attach both adjacent crown formations with a 16-gauge Double ring.

You could substitute two 18-gauge Byzantine jump rings for the 16-gauge Double jump ring, but the second 18-gauge Byzantine ring is quite a bear to get into place. For the sanity of my students, I use a 16-gauge Double ring.

3. Continue attaching the crown formations to a 16-gauge Double ring throughout the length of the chain. The crown formation's outside rings can be untucked to sit on the outside of its neighboring knots in the Byzantine chain, which allows proper flexibility.

4. Start the tapered end triangulation by attaching a 14-gauge ring to the end pair of rings. Then add four 18-gauge jump rings.

5. Attach a second 14-gauge ring to two of the previously added 18-gauge rings, as well as to the second chain's end pair of rings. Then add two more 18-gauge rings.

6. Add a third 14-gauge ring to the two pairs of 18-gauge rings, combining all three 14-gauge rings. Complete the triangulation with a clasp. Finish the opposite end of the Square chain with a 14-gauge triangulation and an additional catch ring.

Square Bead Variation

The Square Bead Variation fills the spaces of the Square design beads that are held in place with beading wire. The wire runs through the 16-gauge connector rings, joining the two chains and cradling a bead between each crown formation. A crimp bead is then smashed onto each wire end to secure the beads. The Square design can be set with either 6mm or 8mm beads. A 6mm bead would sit inside the square hollow, while an 8mm bead would sit on top of the square. A lovely aspect of this design is the balance of its visual geometry.

To set a 7 ½-inch bracelet, you will need thirteen 6mm red tiger's eye beads; two 4mm red tiger's eye beads; two crimp beads; beading wire; and two sets of chain-nose pliers.

1. Cut a length of beading wire that is 1 ½ times longer than the length of the Square chain and add a crimp bead. Loop the wire around the outside, or third, 14-gauge triangulation ring and back through the crimp bead. Run both wires through the pair of 18-gauge rings that joins the first and second 14-gauge triangulation rings.

2. Hold both of the ends of the beading wire in one set of chain-nose pliers and push the crimp bead into the center of the triangulation. Smash the crimp bead, leaving at least 1 inch of beading wire on the short end. Add a 6mm bead to both ends of beading wire. Cut off the excess wire just past the 6mm bead. Don't cut both wires—just one.

3. Run the beading wire through the 16-gauge Double ring and add a second 6mm bead. Continue running the wire through each bead and 16-gauge Double ring.

4. After setting the last 6mm bead, add a crimp bead. Run the beading wire through the base pair of 18-gauge rings, looping it around the third 14-gauge ring and back through the crimp bead, the base pair, and the 6mm bead. Position the crimp bead so that it is cradled inside the triangulation formation. Gently pull the beading wire taut, being careful not to pull the wire too tightly, which will restrict the chain's overall flexibility.

5. After checking the flexibility of the chain (*see* page 51) two or three times and making sure that all of the beads are in place, smash the crimp bead with the chain-nose pliers to secure the beads. Snip off the excess beading wire just inside of the last set of 6mm beads. Be extra careful at this point to cut off only the excess wire and not the main wire holding the beads.

Composed
Designs

This chapter introduces four new intriguing designs: the Diamond, Yin-Yang, Celtic, and Starfish chains, along with their beading variations. Building In complexity, these designs are sure to challenge even the most proficient chain maker and push the veteran crafter to new limits. The Diamond design allows dia-

mond shapes to be built into a Byzantine chain, creating spaces that can be adorned with beads. The Yin-Yang design creates a square formation that when pulled from opposite corners creates two spaces that can also be finished with beads. The Celtic chain allows a length of Byzantine chain to be composed into a large square that has four smaller squares within each Celtic formation. These are then embellished with precious stones. The final design is the Starfish, in which a complete circle of Byzantine chain is pulled inward with five large rings.

Diamond Design

The Diamond design is a length of Byzantine chain that bends and connects at the connector pairs to create a diamond formation. The diamond formation can be used in a number of different ways. A diamond formation can act as a centerpiece by attaching it to a clasp and hanging it from a length of chain, or many diamond formations can be added to a length of chain—as in this choker project. Alternatively, a diamond formation can be built into a length of Byzantine chain to serve as a counterbalance to a larger centerpiece. Whichever path you take, you will have a diamond-shaped space that can be either left open or set with beads (*see* pages 108–109).

To make a 14-inch choker, you will need five hundred and sixteen 18-gauge Byzantine jump rings; three 14-gauge Byzantine catch rings; one clasp; and two pieces of scrap wire.

Diamond Formation

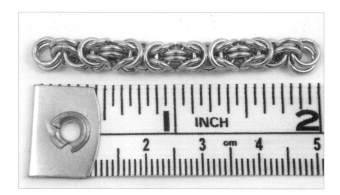

1. Start with a 2-inch length of Byzantine chain made from 46 jump rings. End both sides of the chain with open knot sequences.

2. Lay the chain flat. Fold back and angle open both open knot sequences without twisting the Byzantine chain. The open knot sequences above are held open with two pieces of scrap wire.

3. Add two 18-gauge rings. Attach both folded-back knots to a shared connector pair. This turns the Byzantine chain into a complete circle and creates the diamond formation.

Diamond Design

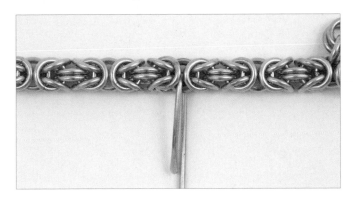

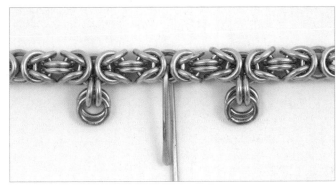

1. Start with a length of Byzantine chain. Identify the center connector pair in the chain and mark it with a piece of scrap wire.

2. Attach two open knot sequences to the Byzantine chain at the second connector pair of both sides from the center. Attach the open knot sequences to only one side of the four-sided chain.

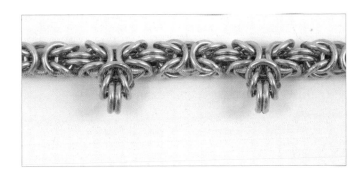

3. Fold back and angle open each open knot sequence and add two rings to create a crown formation (*see* pages 80–81).

4. Attach four rings to each crown formation, creating a second open knot sequence.

5. Fold back and angle open both open knot sequences. The open knot sequences pictured above are held open with two pieces of scrap wire.

6. Attach both knot formations to a shared connector pair to create a complete circle of chain, which is the diamond formation. Make sure you do not twist the chain while combining the knots.

Diamond Bead Variation

Instead of embellishing an entire length of finished chain with beads, each diamond formation (*see* pages 106–107) is set individually. A bead is placed within the diamond-shaped space and then secured with beading wire. The beading wire travels diagonally through the diamond formations and is affixed by looping the ends of the wire around opposite jump rings and then back through a crimp bead on each side of the bead. The crimp beads are then smashed to fasten the bead embellishment.

To set a 14-inch choker, you will need seven 6mm malachite beads; fourteen crimp beads; beading wire; and two sets of chain-nose pliers.

1. Cut a 4-inch piece of beading wire. Run one end of the wire through the top connector pair of the diamond formation, looping it around a single outside ring and back through the connector pair. Then add a crimp bead to both ends of the wire. Hold both ends of the beading wire in one set of chain-nose pliers and push the crimp bead toward the inside of the connector pair. Smash the crimp bead as close to the connector pair as possible, leaving at least 1 inch of beading wire on the short end.

2. Add a 6mm malachite bead to both ends of the beading wire and cut off the excess wire just past the bead. Don't cut both wires—just one. Add a second crimp bead and run the remaining wire through the opposite connector pair.

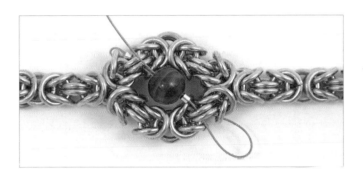

3. Loop the beading wire around a single outside ring and then back through the connector pair, the crimp bead, and the gemstone.

4. Pull the beading wire taut. Do not pull the wire too tightly, as it will restrict the chain's overall flexibility.

5. After checking the chain's flexibility (*see* page 51) and that the bead is snug in the diamond formation, smash the crimp bead with the chain-nose pliers to secure the bead.

6. Snip off the excess beading wire just to the top of the bead. Be extra careful at this point to cut off only the excess wire and not the main wire holding the bead.

Yin-Yang Design

The Yin-Yang design is a Byzantine chain assembled with two crown formations (*see* pages 80–81). The chain is then bent at its connector pairs and formed into a divided rectangle by the crown formations. The two squares within the rectangle are elongated from opposite corners and transform the rectangle into the balanced yin-yang formation. Similar to the Diamond design (*see* pages 106–107), individual yin-yang formations can be combined into a chain pattern or used alone as a centerpiece.

To make an 8-inch bracelet, you will need three hundred and seventy 18-gauge Byzantine jump rings; three 14-gauge Byzantine catch rings; and one clasp.

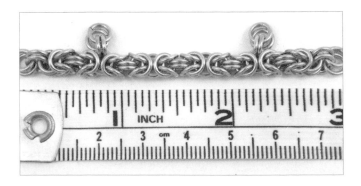

1. Start with a 3-inch length of Byzantine chain made from seventy jump rings. End both sides of the chain with open knot sequences. Attach two open knot sequences to every third connector pair on one side of the four-sided Byzantine chain. You will have five connector pairs between the open knot sequences.

2. Fold back and angle open both open knot sequences into the crown formation. Keep it open by tucking the outside rings of the crown formation into its neighboring knots.

3. Attach both crown formations to a connector pair. Untuck the outside rings of both crown formations so that they lie on top of their neighboring knots within the Byzantine chain.

4. Join the open knot sequences at the end of the Byzantine chain by folding back and adding the connector pair. This creates a divided rectangle with two squares.

5. Attach four 18-gauge rings, assembled 2+2, to the open knot sequences on the two opposite corners of the rectangle. This will elongate the chain and comprise the yin-yang formation.

6. Fold back the crown formation on the opposite corners and add 2 rings to complete the outside crown formations to make the yin-yang formation.

7. If desired, use a connector pair to join multiple yin-yang formations to make a chain. A sequence of four yin-yang formations was used for this project.

Yin-Yang Bead Variation

The Yin-Yang Bead Variation fills the two square-shaped spaces of the yin-yang formation (*see* pages 110–111) with a pair of contrasting beads, which are held in place with beading wire. The beading wire runs through the center of the rectangle's length and through the center connector pairs, cradling the two beads in the yin-yang formation. The ends of the wire are looped and then secured with crimp beads. To capture the visual metaphor of the yin and yang, I chose an asymmetrical freshwater pearl to represent the feminine yin. It is balanced by the metallic shine of the hematite bead, which represents the masculine yang.

To make an 8-inch bracelet, you will need four 6mm hematite beads; four 7mm pearls; eight crimp beads; beading wire; and two sets of chain-nose pliers.

1. Cut a 5-inch piece of beading wire. Run one end through the rectangle's top connector pair. Loop it around a single outside ring and then run it back through the connector pair.

2. Add a crimp bead to both ends of the beading wire and adjust the wire length so that one side is shorter. Hold both ends of the beading wire in one set of chain-nose pliers and push the crimp bead toward the inside of the connector pair. Smash the crimp bead as close to the connector pair as possible, leaving at least 1 inch of beading wire on the short end.

3. Run each end of the beading wire through a 7mm pearl and cut off the excess wire just past the bead. Don't cut both wires—just one.

4. Run the beading wire through the center connector pair into the second square and add a 6mm hematite bead and one crimp bead.

5. Run the beading wire through the connector pair at the rectangle's bottom, keeping the crimp bead just inside the second square.

6. Loop the wire end around a single outside ring and then back through the crimp bead, the connector pair, and the 6mm hematite bead. Pull the beading wire taut, but be careful not to pull it too tightly, which will restrict the overall form.

7. After the flexibility is checked (*see* page 51) and both beads are snug in their squares, smash the crimp bead with chain-nose pliers to secure the beads. Snip off the excess beading wire just inside the 6mm hematite bead. Be extra careful at this point to cut off only the excess wire and not the main wire holding the beads.

Celtic Design

The Celtic design is a length of Byzantine chain assembled with four sequentially placed crown formations (*see* pages 80–81). The chain is then inverted so that all four crown formations face inward. Finally, the finishing pair of jump rings in the crown formations are attached to a 14-gauge Byzantine catch ring to create the Celtic formation. As the Byzantine chain bends at its connector pairs, four small squares are created within one large square that can be filled with beads (*see* pages 116–119), joined into a chain pattern of repeating Celtic formations, or displayed alone as a centerpiece.

To make an 8-inch bracelet, you will need four hundred and eighty 18-gauge Byzantine jump rings (one hundred and twenty for the Celtic formation); six 14-gauge Byzantine catch rings; one clasp; and two pieces of scrap wire.

1. Assemble ninety-four jump rings into a 3 ⁷⁄₈-inch length of Byzantine chain, with both sides ending with open knot sequences. Starting with the second connector pair, add four crown formations, assembled perpendicularly to the Byzantine at every fourth connector pair. All four crowns must be added to the same side of the four-sided Byzantine chain to keep the chain from twisting.

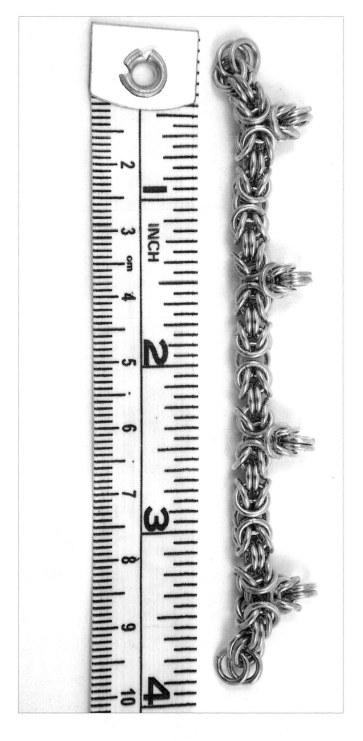

2. With the chain lying flat, fold back and angle open both open knot sequences. Hold the knots open with two pieces of scrap wire.

3. Attach both folded-back knots to a shared connector pair, transforming the Byzantine chain into a square. Try not to twist the chain while combining the knot formations.

4. Invert the square formation so that all four crown formations face inward and the corner connector pairs bend at 90 degrees. You will have a large square composed of four smaller squares. Attach all four crown formations to a 14-gauge catch ring.

Celtic Bead Variation

The Celtic design creates four square-shaped spaces within a large square. These spaces are filled and enhanced with four 6mm beads held in place by a length of beading wire. The beading wire runs throughout the overall Celtic design in an overlapping circle, traveling through the four center crown formations with beads in between. Notice that the overlapping beading wire doubles through two of the beads, with a crimp bead positioned between them. The crimp bead is smashed in place, securing the bead embellishment and complementing each Celtic formation with four 6mm round jade beads.

To set an 8-inch bracelet, you will need sixteen 6mm jade beads; four crimp beads; beading wire; and two sets of chain-nose pliers.

1. Cut a 5-inch piece of beading wire. Run one end through the first pair of rings in the crown formation. Add two 6mm jade beads, one on each end.

2. Run the two ends of the beading wire through the first pair of rings in the adjacent crown formations.

3. On one end of the beading wire, add the third bead. Run the wire through the fourth crown formation. Add the fourth bead and a crimp bead to the other end of the beading wire.

4. Run the free end of the beading wire through the crimp bead in the opposite direction of the first wire to make a loop in the Celtic formation.

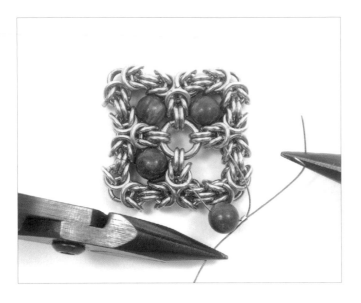

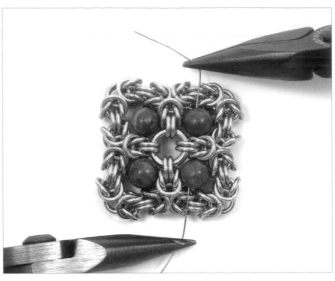

5. Use chain-nose pliers to run the wire ends through the bead.

6. Holding each end of the beading wire with chain-nose pliers, pull the loop tightly so that all four beads fit snugly into their squares without restricting the chain's flexibility. Carefully smash the crimp bead, which sits just inside the crown formation. Snip off any excess wire.

The individual Celtic formations can be joined with 14-gauge Byzantine rings through the corner connector pairs, as shown, to create an angular, repetitive chain design.

As an alternative, each Celtic formation can be joined at two corners as shown, using two 14-gauge Byzantine rings, to create a wide, repetitive chain design.

This single Celtic formation can be utilized as a centerpiece pendant by adding an S-clasp, which allows the length of Byzantine chain to pass through its forged loop.

This single Celtic formation can be used as a key chain by adding a split ring, to hold the keys, inside the circular length of the Byzantine chain.

Starfish Design

To create the Starfish design, five 14-gauge Byzantine rings are added along one side of a Byzantine chain. The chain is then formed into a circle with the five 14-gauge rings pointing inward. Finally, the five jump rings are attached to a 14-gauge jump ring, pulling the circle into a five-pointed starfish formation. Due to this design's width, I recommend using each starfish formation as a centerpiece, which can be set with beads (*see* pages 122–123) or attached to a matching chain.

To make a 15-inch necklace, you will need four hundred and fifty-four 18-gauge Byzantine jump rings (one hundred and twenty for the starfish formation); nine 14-gauge Byzantine catch rings; and one clasp.

1. Assemble one hundred and eighteen jump rings into a 5-inch length of Byzantine chain. End both sides of the chain with open knot sequences. Add five 14-gauge rings to the Byzantine chain at every fourth connector pair, starting with the second connector pair from either end. All five 14-gauge rings must be added to the same side of the four-sided Byzantine in order to keep the chain from twisting.

2. With the chain section lying flat, fold back and angle open both open knot sequences. Make sure you do not twist the Byzantine chain and that all five 14-gauge rings are facing outward. Hold the open knot sequences open with two pieces of scrap wire.

3. Attach both knot formations to a connector pair to create a circle out of the Byzantine chain. Invert the chain so that all five 14-gauge rings face inward.

4. Atach all five 14-gauge rings with a sixth 14-gauge ring, which pulls the circle into the five-pointed starfish formation.

Starfish Bead Variation

The diamond-shaped spaces of the starfish formation can be filled and enhanced with beads. For this centerpiece project, I chose deep purple amethyst beads to complement the beauty of the sterling silver wire. To secure the beads, a length of beading wire is threaded through the perpendicular 14-gauge jump rings inside the design in an overlapping circle. The wire doubles through two of the beads, with a crimp bead positioned between them. The crimp bead is then smashed to secure the bead embellishment.

To set a starfish centerpiece, you will need five 6mm amethyst beads; one crimp bead; beading wire; and two sets of chain-nose pliers.

1. Cut a 5-inch piece of beading wire. Run one end through one 14-gauge jump ring and add a 6mm amethyst bead. Run the wire out the second 14-gauge ring.

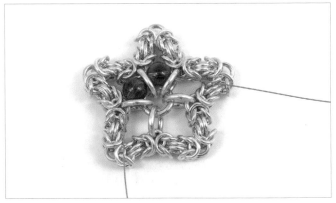

2. Add a second bead. Run the wire through the next 14-gauge ring.

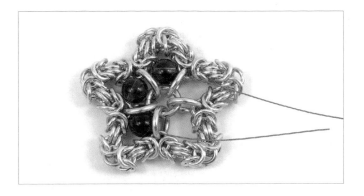

3. Add a third bead. Run the wire through the next 14-gauge jump ring.

4. Add a fourth bead. Run the wire through the next 14-gauge ring.

5. Add the fifth bead and one crimp bead.

6. Run the free end of the beading wire through the crimp bead and the fifth bead in the opposite direction from the other wire to complete a full loop.

7. Use chain-nose pliers to run the wire ends through their neighboring bead. Holding both ends of the beading wire with chain-nose pliers, pull the loop of wire tightly so that all five beads fit snugly in their spaces and do not restrict the chain's overall flexibility. Carefully smash the crimp bead, as it will sit slightly inside one of the 14-gauge rings. Snip off any excess wire.

This starfish formation can be used as a centerpiece pendant by adding an S-clasp and attaching the clasp to a Byzantine chain.

Glossary

Anneal: To heat metal to a prescribed temperature, then allowing it to cool slowly, which reduces the stress in the metal.

B & S: Abbreviation for Brown and Sharpe, the individuals who developed a common standard for measuring round wire.

Beading wire: Multistranded stainless steel wires that are braided and nylon coated, used for setting semiprecious stones.

Bi-crown design: Original Byzantine chain pattern enhanced with sequentially placed crown formations built onto every connector pair onto two sides of the chain, which allows beads to be set between.

Burr: A thin ridge or area of roughness produced by the serrating action of cutting metal wire with side cutters.

Caliper: A measuring instrument with one fixed jaw and one adjustable jaw, used especially to measure diameter or thickness.

Catch ring: A single ring, or length of, 14-gauge rings attached to the end of the Byzantine chain that allows the clasp to catch on and secure the bracelet.

Celtic design: Original Byzantine chain design that allows four diamond forms to combine into one larger square that can be filled with stone beads.

Charm: A small ornament, typically cast of pewter or fine metal, with a loop for attaching to a bracelet with a jump ring.

Circumference: The length of the outside perimeter of a circle.

Clasp: A hook-shaped device designed for grasping the catch ring to hold the bracelet securely together.

Coil: A linear tube created by wrapping wire around a mandrel in a spiral course.

Connector pair: A pair of two rings that remain parallel to one another, sequentially placed between each knot formation in the Byzantine chain.

Crimp beads: Tiny silver tubes utilized by being smashed around two threads of beading wire in order to hold beads in place in a chain.

Crown design: Original Byzantine chain pattern enhanced with sequentially placed crown formations built onto every other connector pair onto one side of the chain, which allows beads to be set between.

Diameter: The thickness of a wire or mandrel determined by measuring with a caliper; the length of a straight line through the center of a circular object.

Diamond design: Original Byzantine pattern that is joined in a circle, bending at its connector pair, creating a diamond-shaped form to be filled with stone beads.

Double burr: A small (double-burred) piece of metal removed by flush-cutting 14-gauge jump rings. *See* Flush-cutting on page 34.

End connector pair: A pair of two rings; same as a normal connector pair, yet this pair is at the end of the chain length.

Flush: Having or forming a continuous plane or unbroken surface; arranged edge to edge so as to fit snugly; closing the jump ring edges together without gaps.

Gargoyle head: A sharp burr of metal on a jump ring made by cutting past one ring and nicking the next.

Gauge: A measurement of the thickness or diameter of sheet metal and round wire.

Half-Square design: Original combined chain design based on hanging the Crown design from a sequence of large 14-gauge rings.

Jump ring: A full circle of metal wire that has been cut off a coil, thus offsetting the ends of the jump ring due to the wrapping action of the coil.

Knot formation: A formation of four rings that are folded back and angled open to reveal a rectangular opening in which two more rings are added in order to create the Byzantine chain.

Large Knot design: Original additive chain design in which an 18-gauge knot formation is replaced by a larger 14-gauge knot formation.

Large Ring design: Original linear chain design in which a single 14-gauge ring is added between two sections of Byzantine chain for the purpose of adding charms to a bracelet.

Mandrel: A round metal bar that serves as a core around which material, such as metal wire, may be cast, molded, forged, or bent.

Open knot sequence: This formation is created when the Byzantine chain ends with six rings, combined in three pairs of two rings, and added 2+2+2. The first pair is the connector pair and the next two pairs have the potential to be folded back and angled open into a Knot formation.

Perpendicular: A geometric relation of two lines or objects that are located at right angles (90 degrees) to each other or to the plane of the horizon.

Pi: The 16th letter of the Greek alphabet, pronounced 'pie,' and representing the number 3.14159. . . This number is utilized in geometry as the ratio of a circle's circumference to its diameter.

Semiprecious stones: A group of gemstones that have less commercial value than a precious stone, including amethyst, carnelian, hematite, jade, lapis lazuli, serpentine, turquoise, and many more.

Sequential: A following of one thing after another in a continuous succession. It refers to the descriptive title of the sequential Byzantine chain, where knot formations are spaced between each connector pair in a continuous pattern.

Side Knot design: Original additive chain design, which allows for the Large Knot formation to be turned 45 degrees in relation to and combined into the Byzantine chain.

Square design: Original combined chain design that allows two Byzantine chains to form a sequence of square-shaped negative spaces to be filled with stone beads.

Yin-Yang design: Original combined chain design that allows the Byzantine chain to form two offset diamond-shaped spaces to be filled with stone beads.

Wave design: Original combined chain design that allows a section to be built from a Byzantine chain at every fourth connector pair and then attached back to the original chain with 14-gauge jump rings.

Wrapping: To wind metal wire around a mandrel in order to form a linear coil of the same diameter as the mandrel.

Resources

Listed below are some manufacturers and suppliers for many of the materials used in this book. Most sell their products exclusively to craft and jewelry supply retailers, which are a consumer's most dependable source for chain-making supplies. If you can't find a store in your area that carries a particular item, a manufacturer can direct you to the nearest retailer.

Handtool and Bead Suppliers

Rio Grande in Albuquerque, NM
1-800-545-6566
www.riogrande.com

Fire Mt. Gems in Grants Pass, OR
1-800-423-2319
www.firemountaingems.com

House of Tools Co.
780-944-9988

Lacy West Supplies LTD in Vancouver, BC, Canada
1-604-669-5229

Wire Suppliers

Silver, gold (precious metals)

Rio Grande in Albuquerque, NM
1-800-545-6566
www.riogrande.com

Hauser & Miller in St. Louis, MO
1-800-462-7447

TSI in Seattle, WA
1-800-426-9984

Brass, NuGold, copper, nickel-silver wire (base metals)

E. B. Fitler & Co in Milton, DE
1-800-346-2497

Wheeler Industrial Corporation in Irvington, NJ
973-926-0551
www.wheelermetal4u.com

Integrated Nonferrous Metals Company in Waterbury, CT
860-274-7255
www.redmetals.com

Eagle Alloys
1-800-237-9012
www.eaglealloys.com

Precut Jump Rings

Fire Mt. Gems in Grants Pass, OR
1-800-423-2319
www.firemountaingems.com

Miscellaneous

www.discshoppe.com
206-372-4747
Frisbee golf discs

Publications

Art Jewelry
www.artjewelrymag.com

Lapidary Journal
www.lapidaryjournal.com

American Craft Magazine
www.craftcouncil.org

Metalsmith Magazine
write to:
The Society of North American Goldsmiths
710 East Ogden Ave. Suite 600
Naperville, IL 60563–8603

Author Contact

Scott David Plumlee
DavidChainJewelry
www.davidchain.com

Acknowledgments

I wish to dedicate this book to everyone who believed in me, especially:

- My loving parents, Larry and Shirley, for their encouragement and support

- My brother Jeff and his wife Erika, for making me an uncle twice

- All the students who took workshops and encouraged me to write this book

- All the patrons who purchased my jewelry art and invested in my business

- All the teaching institutions that invited me to lead chain-making workshops

- All the fine art retail galleries that retailed my jewelry and provided exposure

- Glasshouse Gallery and Lucia Douglas gallery for the exposure

- The editorial crew at Watson-Guptill for their patience and direction

- Lisa Eastman for the amazing step-by-step photography work

- Linda Nathan, Julie Baker, Daphne Page, and Shirley Plumlee for proofreading

- Adobe and Macromedia for creating such amazing, flawless software

Scott David Plumlee is an authority on ancient chain designs. He has created more than sixty unique chain designs based on mathematical formulas. His chain-making workshops have been presented throughout Washington State. He now lives in Manhattan, Kansas.

Index